BRAM STOKER'S

Francis Ford Coppola and James V. Hart

BRAM STOKER'S

BRAM STOKER'S

Dracula

The Film and the Legend

Directed by Francis Ford Coppola
Screenplay by James V. Hart

Afterword by Leonard Wolf

Photographs of the film by Ralph Nelson

Edited by Diana Landau

A NEWMARKET PICTORIAL MOVIEBOOK

Newmarket Press · New York

Features about the cast, crew, and filmmaking process are based in part on production notes by Katherine Orloff and transcripts of interviews by Jeff Werner, Davia Nelson, and Susan Dworkin.

Credits and acknowledgments of permissions for illustrations and excerpts from other works are found on page 172.

This book published simultaneously in the United States of America and in Canada.

92   93   94   95   10 9 8 7 6 5 4 3 2 1

Library of Congress Cataloguing-in-Publication Data

Coppola, Francis Ford, 1939-
    Bram Stoker's Dracula: the film and the legend / Francis Ford Coppola and James V. Hart.
    p.   cm. — (A Newmarket pictorial moviebook)
The official pictorial book tie-in to the film Bram Stoker's Dracula, including the complete screenplay.
    Includes bibliographical references.
    ISBN 1-55704-140-7   ISBN 1-55704-139-3 (pbk.)
    1. Bram Stoker's Dracula (Motion picture)   I. Hart, James V.
II. Bram Stoker's Dracula (Motion picture)   III. Title.   IV. Series.
PN1997.B72223B7   1992
791.43'72—dc20   92-28191
                                          CIP

Quantity Purchases

Companies, professional groups, clubs, and other organizations may qualify for special terms when ordering quantities of this title. For information, write Special Sales, Newmarket Press, 18 East 48th Street, New York, N.Y. 10017, or call (212) 832-3575.

Editorial, design, and production services by Walking Stick Press, San Francisco:
    Diana Landau, editor; Linda Herman, book design; Robert Cornish, design associate.

Newmarket Productions staff: Esther Margolis, director; Keith Hollaman, editor;
    Walter Friedman, production.

Manufactured in the United States of America

First Edition

Other Newmarket Pictorial Moviebooks include:

The Age of Innocence: A Portrait of the Film

Dances With Wolves: The Illustrated Story of the Epic Film

Far and Away: The Illustrated Story of a Journey from Ireland to America in the 1890s

The Inner Circle: An Inside View of Soviet Life Under Stalin

City of Joy: The Illustrated Story of the Film

Gandhi: A Pictorial Biography

Cover photographs by Ralph Nelson

Contents

Finding the Vampire's Soul

by Francis Ford Coppola

My biggest problem—YOU CAN'T JUST DO IT AGAIN.

Italicized passages are from Francis Coppola's
production journal for *Bram Stoker's Dracula*

Above: *Francis Ford Coppola.* Right: *Poster by Albin Grau for F. W. Murnau's* Nosferatu.

I think the first Dracula film I ever saw was the John Carradine *House of Dracula.* I adored Carradine, with his gaunt face and how he would actually lift his cape and turn into a bat—he is my prototype Dracula. But as I look back, although I was a fan of all those early horror pictures, the great one to me was *Bride of Frankenstein. Dracula* I liked a little less, but more than *The Mummy.*

Murnau's *Nosferatu,* from 1922, is probably the greatest film made on the Dracula story. It was actually an unauthorized version, and Stoker's widow sued the filmmakers. It's a very powerful movie, a masterpiece that probed the strange part of us that's obsessed with vampires. But it's a very free retelling of the story, with the setting moved to Bremen, Germany, and many plot elements that differ from the novel. It has Dracula bringing the plague to Bremen, which isn't in the book at all—though Stoker does liken the blood disease Dracula infects his victims with to a plague.

I saw the 1931 Bela Lugosi version when I was a little older, maybe fourteen. I loved Lugosi, and especially the part where Harker first goes to the castle and meets Dracula.

Those scenes are the greatest part of the story, in the book or any of the movies. But I remember being disappointed by the three Brides—they were just standing there in their robes, looking dead, and that wasn't what a fourteen-year-old boy wants to see.

I always liked Lon Chaney as the Wolfman because he felt bad afterwards, and he had a lot of nobility.

I had read the book when I was pretty young and loved it. Then as a teenager, I was the drama counselor at a camp in upstate New York, and had a bunk of eight- and nine-year-old boys. I would read aloud to them at night, and one summer we read *Dracula.* And when we got to that chilling moment —when Harker looks out the window and sees Dracula crawling across the face of the wall like a bug— even those little boys knew, this was going to be good! And you know, the book doesn't get any better than that.

I liked it that in those early scenes

the Count was telling Harker stories about old wars and such. I remember as a kid going to the *Encyclopaedia Britannica* to look up Dracula—and there he was, Vlad the Impaler. I read about this fierce guy, how he literally stopped the Turks by impaling his own people on stakes, and I was just thrilled to think that he really existed.

I would like our filmmaking to give Dracula his due in terms of his place in history—that he was considered an extremely modern Renaissance prince and very brilliant. He was an extraordinary figure. So we use this to ground our fantasy, as Bram Stoker did.

When I read Jim's script, I thought he had made a brilliant innovation by using that history of Prince Vlad to set the frame for the whole story. It was closer to Stoker's novel than anything done before. Also, I felt immediately that he had written it as a story of passion and eroticism—the Brides weren't just standing around; they actually raped Harker—and that filled my child's heart with enthusiasm.

Mainly, it was that no one had ever done the book. I'm amazed, watching all the other Dracula films, how much they held back from what was written or implied, how they played havoc with the characters and their relationships. In our movie, the characters resemble Stoker's in their personalities and function, including many characters that are often cut out. And then the whole last section of the book—when Van Helsing is uncovering Dracula's weaknesses, and the Vampire Killers pursue him back to his castle in Transylvania, and the whole thing climaxes in an enormous John Ford shootout—no one has ever portrayed that.

Aside from the one innovative take that comes from history—the love story between Mina and the Prince—we were scrupulously true to the book.

The movie is going to tell itself like the novel: with all the journals and letters leading up to some dreadful thing. It's very suspenseful and it also helps get the audience around.

Stoker composed his novel in an innovative way: as though it were a compilation of

```
d. VIEW ON DOOR
   Holmwood rushes in in his hat and topcoat.  PULL BACK to see
   Van Helsing tying off Lucy's arm in her state of undress.
                        HOLMWOOD
              --What the bloody hell?!  What
              are you doing to my Lucy!
   He grabs at Van Helsing.  Seward pulls him back.  Van
   Helsing looks at Seward, then at Holmwood.  He "sees"
   everything.
                        SEWARD
              He's trying to save her, Art.
              Professor Van Helsing knows more
              about obscure diseases than any
              man in the world!
e. MED. CLOSE SHOT VAN HELSING
                        VAN HELSING
                     (calm, in charge)
              The young miss is very bad.
f. VIEW ON HOLWOOD
   Seward at his side.
```

notes and journals and fragments of diaries he had pieced together. So as you read the book, it's like he's saying, look, we have these fragments: judge for yourself whether this was true.

In the montage where Harker arrives in Transylvania, we've used lots of period documents and travel aids. The journey into Transylvania is unveiled in layers, in multiple dreamlike images and writings, snippets of documentation. Finally the letter from Dracula takes us across to the other side. . . .

We're trying stylistically to create our own impression, an image that flows like a tapestry, undulating like a dream. When you think of the clothes and the beautiful fabrics, and put them on a couple of main characters—that is the set.

After I had read the script, I had a couple of takes about this film. First, I wanted it to have a very young, talented, attractive cast. Second, and related to the first, I wanted to lead with the costumes, let them be the jewel of the show. Rather than tax the

Top: *The director with cinematographer Michael Ballhaus.* Above: *Coppola's annotations on the script.*

COPPOLA AS DIRECTOR: THE IDEAL AND THE REAL

When Francis Coppola agreed to direct Bram Stoker's *Dracula*, screenwriter James Hart had found his deliverer. "Francis is a writer. He is steeped in literature. He's a historian, an inventor, a man who has one foot in the nineteenth century and another in the twentieth. He understands structure—how hard it is to get those scenes to work on paper and that they don't just show up the first time."

Hart admitted to the director in their first meeting that he had borrowed many of his techniques in writing the script. "I learned so much from watching his movies—about intercutting, parallel action, the ability to telescope using fades in and out. Also about the use of language, voiceovers spoken over the scene, and a stylized use of violence that is never gratuitous but has enormous impact. He's used all these elements extensively in *Dracula*."

With *Dracula*, Coppola returns to the horror genre that marked his

entry into the feature film world: in 1963 he wrote and directed *Dementia 13*. His most recent film is *Godfather III*, the last episode in the much-honored three-part chronicle of the Corleone family. Coppola's other credits include the *Life Without Zoe* episode of *New York Stories, Tucker: The Man and His Dream, Gardens of Stone, Peggy Sue Got Married, Cotton Club, Rumblefish, The Outsiders, One From the Heart, Apocalypse Now*, and *The Conversation*.

There are two sides of him, Coppola says: "the guy who loves the actors, and the guy who loves when the fader brings up a red light." He has the reputation of being an intuitive director with actors, who appreciate his methods. "He is a genius, I think," says Anthony Hopkins. "He creates a great atmosphere to work in and tremendous power on the screen. All the shots are set up, but he improvises within that, and talks you through the scenes. He seems to conjure stuff up out of nothing."

Gary Oldman adds, "I've enjoyed working with Francis tremendously—on the floor, in the moment, he's at his best. Someone once said, and it's true, that it's like he knows what the characters are thinking."

Coppola notes, "I was a drama counselor with kids, and I still like to take the actors up to the country and find new ways to work together— do theater games, improvisations, read the book aloud, stage scenes and discuss characters— always try to make the day interesting.

"But ultimately, with all the preparation you do, and all the love and support and coaching, you're really trying to catch lightning in a bottle. You're saying, 'Okay, go jump off the cliff,' and you hope the actor does it. To get that, I think you have to allow and encourage actors to improvise—to know the text and the meaning but then use their own feelings to express it. And when you get it, it's thrilling. It's really the act of creation.

"But I love the technological side too—the fader and the red light, I need some of that. I was this nine-year-old with a television and a movie projector and a tape recorder, and I was obsessed with remote control."

Walking the tightrope between creativity and control had its challenges in *Dracula*, as Coppola urged his collaborators to stretch beyond their usual ways of achieving results. "You want people to know how you feel about a story, and if everyone expresses how they feel through the approved vocabulary, then the audience won't have your feeling because it will be like everyone else's.

"I'm always trying to be very clear about what I want, so that the bureaucracy I depend on doesn't edit my ideas. A team of filmmakers is like a garden in which every variety of plant is overproducing. The art department tries to tell the whole movie in sets. The cinematographer tries to tell it in lighting. The make-up specialist is trying to do the whole thing with makeup and beasts. Each actor wants to tell the whole story with his character.

"The director has to smush all this brilliant creativity together and make it work. The director is the place where the real and the ideal come together."

Coppola directs Gary Oldman in the final scene.

resources of the production with elaborate sets, I wanted to make a more imaginative use of space and shadow.

We have tried for a unique, striking visual style that immediately says you are in the realm of magic. We explored the tradition of early cinema, the era when magicians first brought cinema to the world—which was the period when Stoker wrote *Dracula*. So we have used many of those naive effects, tricks done with the camera or with mirrors, to give the film almost a mythical soul.

I always had the idea that when you were in the presence of a vampire, the laws of physics didn't work quite right: maybe the earth didn't rotate at the same speed, or things defied gravity. And I knew that vampires hold sway over shadows, so the shadows have a life of their own.

Dracula's oath to evil in the Prologue: This has to be very powerful, so we understand how the highest angel can turn into the most base devil by a simple act of renouncement.

Doing justice to the complex character of Dracula was one of our main goals. He's been portrayed as a monster or as a seducer, but knowing his biography made me think of him as a fallen angel, as Satan. The irony is that he was a champion of the church, this hero who singlehandedly stopped the Turks, and then he renounced God because his wife was a suicide and was denied holy burial. When great ones fall, they become the most powerful devils—Satan was once the highest angel.

Man's relationship with God is sacramental; it's expressed through the symbol of blood. So when Dracula rejects God, blood becomes the basis for all kinds of unholy sacraments in the story: baptism, marriage, the Mass. . . .

My father used to say an old Italian thing: that you should never put an infant in the room with an old person during the night, because without being able to help it, the old person will be sucking the life out of it. . . . Dracula represents an extraordinary phenomenon: the idea that even when dead you can draw on the vital life force—blood—and emerge on the other side of life in this evil, predatory form.

I would like to do Dracula like a dark, passionate, erotic dream. Above all, it is a love story between Dracula and Mina . . . souls reaching out through a universe of horror and pathos. The counterforce to all this is Harker, the husband. And the subordinating characters: Van Helsing, Quincey, Seward, and Lucy are all interacting as lovers and partners in the story.

Blood is also the symbol of human passion, the source of all passion. I think that is the main subtext in our story. We've tried to depict feelings so strong they can survive across the centuries, like Dracula's love for Mina/Elizabeth. The idea that love can conquer death, or worse than death—that she can actually give back to the vampire his lost soul. One of the main reasons we cast Gary Oldman in the role is that he was clearly capable of expressing this depth of passion in his acting.

Usually Dracula is just a reptilian creature in a horror film. I want people to understand the historical and literary traditions behind the story. To see that underneath this vampire myth is really fundamental human stuff that everyone feels and knows.

Blood is the primary metaphor. In *Nosferatu* Murnau saw the connection between the vampire's diseased blood and plague; people today may see, as we did, the connection with AIDS. Even if people today don't feel a sacramental relationship with God, I think they can understand how many people renounce their blood ties to the creation—to the creative spirit, or whatever it is—and become like living dead. The vampire has lost his soul, and that can happen to anyone.

Dracula's vampire brides in the 1931 Tod Browning/Universal Pictures Dracula.

5

The Script That Wouldn't Die

by James V. Hart

Jim Hart on the Castle Dracula set.

"**W**hy?" the producer asked, wishing he'd never taken this meeting with a fortysomething, graying, unproduced writer (me). "Why do a remake of *Dracula?* It's been done a hundred times? Everybody knows the story. Hell, there's a Muppet Count Dracula that teaches kids to count!"

My response was always the same: because the real *Dracula* has never been done. Anyone who has read Bram Stoker's brilliant, erotic, Gothic novel can understand that my answer was not meant to be arrogant, but rather reverent of Stoker's literary classic.

First published in 1897, *Dracula* was generally panned by critics. Stoker, the rather stiff, reserved manager of London's famed Lyceum Theatre, never achieved the critical stature he deserved; "hack" was a word often used to describe his talents. Yet *Dracula* has never been out of print since it first appeared. It can be found in every library in America and on the paperback shelves of most bookstores.

I first read it on a plane from France to New York in April 1977. One scene I found so intensely erotic and diabolically evil that I passed out right in my foie gras. Back home in New York that night, I became so overwrought while reading that I threw the book in my wardrobe and slammed the door. Later that night, around 2:00 a.m., my wife awoke to my face leering over her, watching the jugular pump seductively on her neck. I was hooked.

✠

"The power of the vampire is that people do not believe he exists." So says Dr. Abraham Van Helsing, the fearless vampire killer in Stoker's tale of blood and lust. Certainly there have been enough movie portrayals of the vampire to convince us that he must exist—but few of them have shown his power.

My first exposure was through the ghoulishly campy Dracula films from England's Hammer Studios, starring Christopher Lee as the Count and Peter Cushing as Van Helsing. In this country, Roger Corman and others produced low-budget vampire quickies, shown mostly on drive-in double bills where most of the action was in the backseat. I freely admit that my own first effort at a vampire screen treatment was titled *Pom-pom Girls Meet the Wolfman*, in which a squad of voluptuous vampire cheerleaders encounter the Wolfman during homecoming weekend.

I don't mean to suggest that Christopher Lee does not hold a respected place in vampire film lore. The infamous Hammer productions of the 1960s and '70s certainly kept the legendary Count alive.

Eventually I caught up with Tod Browning's 1931 *Dracula* for Universal Pictures, the Bela Lugosi standard that had caused people to faint in the aisles. I also saw Louis Jourdan give the Count a try in the 1976 BBC miniseries (with Frank Finlay as Van Helsing). And I was impressed with Frank Langella's interpretation on Broadway, which brought a sexual energy to the character never before seen.

As I watched in the opening night audience, a woman seated in front of me whispered (quite loudly) a phrase I have never forgotten: "I'd rather spend one night with Dracula, dead, than the rest of my life with my husband, alive!"

That telling remark convinced me that none of the previous film incarnations had done justice to Stoker's unnerving, sexually charged novel and its tragic hero. For *Dracula* to be done right on the screen, it needed a magnificent production on an epic scale, and a reading that reached to the heart of the character's seductiveness.

Women more than men have tended to read *Dracula* and other vampire stories, and to understand the vampire's attraction. Vampires offer a delectable alternative to the drudgery of mortal life and the promises of religion. They offer immortality here and now—life after death that you can take to the bank, because you can see it in action right before your eyes. You don't have to take a chance on going to heaven or hell; you can live forever right here on earth. Leonard Wolf, whose *The Annotated Dracula* is required reading for vampophiles, refers to this death-cheating bargain as "the infinitely stopped moment."

✠

In 1977 with the help of a Texas partner, I began my attempt to bring *Dracula* to the screen. The first thing I did was to seek out Leonard Wolf, then head of the English Department at San Francisco State University,

and engage his services. After talking for an hour over lunch, I knew that if I ever took a meeting with the devil, I wanted Wolf there to hold my hand. Born in Transylvania, he has made extensive studies of Dracula and vampires in general, and his insights on their psychological appeal are acute. We vowed allegiance and toiled mightily, but never came up with the right screenplay to bring Dracula to life. But Leonard opened a window for me that would never close.

Every two or three years thereafter, as my career sputtered and flashed "potential," agents would ask me what I was passionate about doing as a movie. I always responded "*Dracula*," and coffins would slam in my face. Finally in 1990, producers Robert O'Connor and Michael Apted actually read the book and said, "Let's make a deal."

With their support and the conviction of cable TV executive Karen Moore, I was fortunate to get paid enough to write the script that had been burning inside me since the day I read Stoker. And by then I had enough screenwriting experience to put it together.

As I worked, I couldn't help thinking about who might translate the story onto the screen as director. Because I had always seen the novel as a sweeping epic romance, my first choice was David Lean. More than one movie executive laughed when I mentioned this dream aloud, but I was serious. *Dracula* is not about a guy in a tuxedo. It is a story with rich literary and historical dimensions (see the sidebar about the historical Dracula in the Prologue), and it needed the kind of director who could realize them.

✠

Frank Langella in the 1977 Broadway revival of the Balderston-Deane adaptation of Dracula, *with sets and costumes by Edward Gorey.*

If Bram Stoker had not written *Dracula*, he would survive merely as a literary footnote to the the Victorian age. Though he authored sixteen other books, only *Dracula* rises above the ordinary to stand as a classic—at once a terrifying Gothic adventure, a dark mirror of Victorian obsessions, and a portrait of psychic conflicts that have plagued humankind eternally.

Born in Dublin in 1847, Stoker was a sickly child whose mother entertained him with Irish ghost stories. He compensated by becoming a star athlete and honor student at Trinity University, and took a civil service job after graduating, but became fascinated with the theater; for a time he was drama critic for the *Dublin Mail*. He loved Walt Whitman's poetry and championed feminist causes, a position he later reversed.

In 1796 Stoker met the famed actor Sir Henry Irving, "his real-life vampire," as George Stade notes, who would dominate the rest of his life. Stoker became the manager of Irving's Lyceum Theatre in London and labored tirelessly in this job for nearly 30 years—still finding time to write his fiction and earn a law degree.

Gothic horror had been a popular genre in England since the early 19th century. Stoker was an enthusistic practitioner, and when he decided to attempt a vampire tale, he had several models: *Varney the Vampyre*, a potboiler serial; Sheridan LeFanu's more sophisticated *Carmilla*, and especially John Polidori's *The Vampyre*. The last novel has a fascinating genesis: in 1816, during a rainy sojourn at Lake Geneva, a group of literary lights—Lord Byron, Percy Shelley and his wife-to-be Mary, and Polidori, who was Byron's doctor—amused each other with scary stories. Mary Shelley's became the seminal *Frankenstein*, and Polidori's *The Vampyre* caused a mild sensation when published, largely because its fiendish protagonist resembled Byron.

Stoker made good use of these models, and of vampire folklore, but his real innovation in *Dracula* was his discovery of the bloodthirsty 15th-century Transylvanian prince, Vlad Tepes, to ground the novel historically. His other innovation, constructing the story in the form of "contemporaneous" letters and journals, has also been praised. But while *Dracula* was a popular success from the start, it did not find favor with the critics of its day.

After nearly a century in print, however, and countless theatrical and film adaptations, *Dracula* is seen in a different light. In its barely veiled eroticism, we recognize Stoker's troubled reaction to his own libido and especially that of women. We still thrill to his vivid descriptions of horrifying and supernatural events. And in his deathless creation, the king vampire Dracula, we find "something at once monstrous and definitively human," touching on our fears of death and the lure of immortality; the seduction of power and control; the struggle to define the bounds of sexuality; the fight between the forces of day and night, light and dark, rationality and blind impulse, fantasy and reality.

Top: *Bram Stoker, photographed in 1906.* Above: *Original manuscript of Stoker's first title page, using the title* The Un-dead.

In November of 1990 I received a phone call from my agent, informing me that Francis Ford Coppola was prepared to direct my screenplay of *Dracula*. From cable TV movie to "Francis Ford Coppola Presents"? Even as I write this line I can hardly believe it. I quietly thanked Leonard Wolf for opening the window, and David Lean in spirit for leading me to the perfect director—my own generation's master filmmaker.

So how did this filmmaking legend get involved with such genre fare? It was due to the nineteen-year-old Winona Ryder, who had read my screenplay and became my champion. Miss Ryder asked Francis for his reaction to the script, as she was interested in the role of Mina and valued his opinion. Fortunately for this screenwriter—and for filmgoers—Coppola's opinion was that Winona absolutely should play Jonathan Harker's bride-to-be and the object of Dracula's long-lost love. And, by the way, could he direct the film?

Francis and I met to begin work in March 1991, with the help of his research assistant, Anahid Nazarian, our valued partner in examining and analyzing the screenplay. In our first meeting, I realized how much I had learned about film storytelling techniques from the man sitting before me. Without knowing it, he had influenced the writing of this screenplay—his famous baptism/massacre montage in *The Godfather Part I*, for example—and I confessed as much to him.

The rest, as they say, is history. Francis assembled an extraordinary cast and crew to execute our mutual vision. Eiko Ishioka's unique costumes are practically sets in themselves. Michael Ballhaus's cinematography evokes the masters of classic black-and-white films—but in riveting color. Tom Sanders's production designs and Garrett Lewis's set dressings complement Coppola's vivid imagery.

Greg Cannom's special makeup effects do not rely on computers and morphing, yet inflict on us a bounty of primordial scares. Roman Coppola, Michael Lantieri, and the special effects crew also eschewed sophisticated computer technology and made this one the old-fashioned way, in the tradition of Griffith, Murnau, Dreyer, Welles, and the other great early filmmakers. There isn't room to elaborate on the wonderful performances—but wait until you see Gary Oldman's portrayal of the warrior prince Dracula!

The result of all their efforts is a motion picture production of *Dracula* like nothing we have seen. As directed by Coppola, it is a lush epic in the David O. Selznick vein, but with contemporary sexual underpinnings and stylized bloodspilling. Like all of Coppola's best work, it also has echoes of great opera.

A produced screenplay is a collaboration and this one notably so, as I hope I've made clear. This book contains the screenplay that the movie industry said was dead before it was even written . . . the screenplay that Winona Ryder shocked her agents and career shapers by committing to, and then committed Francis . . . the screenplay that Leonard Wolf and I could not crack for all those years but never gave up on. That it can now appear in this form is due to all of them and many others—and to the enduring life force of Bram Stoker's story and its star. You just can't keep a good vampire down.

Dracula's Guest *was the first of three story collections published posthumously. The title story was later adapted for the film* Dracula's Daughter *(see Afterword).*

Prologue

The Wolf of Christendom

Close shot

A large cross. We hear sounds of battle; fire illuminates the sky. Professor Van Helsing reads the following legend in voiceover:

"The year, 1462. Constantinople had fallen. Moslem Turks swept into Europe with a vast, superior force, striking at Roumania, threatening all of Christendom."

The cross crumbles and a crescent is raised in its place. *Track in on map of Transylvania.* Legend continues:

"From Transylvania arose a Roumanian knight of the Sacred Order of the Dragon— Vlad the Impaler, known as Draculea."

Insert—a fist gripping the hilt of a sword

A flag bearing a crusader's cross appears behind sword. Legend continues:

"A renowned military genius, his blood-thirsty ways were notorious throughout Europe. In a bold surprise attack, he led 7,000 of his countrymen against 30,000 Turks in a last heroic attempt to save his homeland and the Holy Church."

We pan across Dracula's crest, across the details of the battle plan—crosses against crescents. We hear the sounds of battle: thundering horses, clash of steel, men yelling . . . dying . . .

[Transylvania battleground—silhouette]

We see in profile a warrior prince being blessed by a priest. He puts on his helmet, which is fashioned like a great wolf's head. Prince Dracula.

Right: *Storyboard art by Peter Ramsey for the opening battle sequence, Prince Vlad impaling a Turkish soldier.* Opposite: *Dracula bursts into the castle chapel in search of his princess.*

Wide shot

Dracula attacking a Turk. He impales him. We track into Dracula's face, and he lifts a wooden pike with the Turk into the air. Pan across a field of impaled Turks; one of them, in closeup, slowly slides down the stake. Legend continues:

"15,000 Turks were slaughtered. Prince Dracula ordered all wounded and prisoners to be impaled—a message to the enemies of the cross of Christ. The Turkish army fled in horror at the barbarous sight."

On the Turks

as they flee; crescents and banners fall from the horizon in retreat.

Francis Coppola's notes planning the battle scene, after a recent viewing of Kurosawa's *Kagemusha:*

"Right to left, soldiers on mountain range with spears. There's fog and some foreground flags and men crouching down. It's possible the whole battle could be done with an artificial sun behind the moving shadows of the men. . . . There are some spectacular red sunset shots with the troops emerging over the crest of the hill. The shapes of their helmets against the sky. . . . What about people on cliffs with dramatic Carpathian Alps in front projection?. . . Night, high winds, fabrics blowing in the wind. The sound of the fabric."

Wide high angle
Dracula surrounded by his men. They realize they are victorious. His face becomes illuminated as we slowly move into a close-up as he kneels, removing his wolf helmet. He kisses his crucifix.

DRACULA
(Roumanian)
God be praised—I am victorious.

Anguished cries echo around him. He stares at the fresh blood on his own hands, as if seeing it for the first time. A woman screams offscreen. He pales. A horrible premonition seizes him. The dark cloud of black smoke passes over him, casting him into shadow.

We barely see the faint image of a woman's face—falling, falling. It dissolves away . . .

DRACULA
(desperate, dreading)
Elisabeta . . !

[Open country—night]

Wide shot
Dracula in silhouette is racing across the screen. We see impaled Turks lined up along the road—his castle in the distance. We tilt down to reveal: wolves hungrily approaching a dying Turk in the foreground. Voiceover resumes:

"A Turkish arrow carried a deceitful message to Dracula's bride, Elizabeth. Believing he had been killed in battle, she flung herself from the castle turret."

[Castle chapel—night]

Close shot
Dracula enters, running through the door. (Music cue: chanting prayer.)

Dracula's POV—track into Elizabeth
Her wet, regal, lifeless body twisted and bent beneath a great stone dragon arch before a shrine of the crucifixion.

Low angle shot—Elizabeth in foreground
Dracula crumbles prostrate over her. We track in on him. The warrior in him fails,

Opposite: *Elizabeth lies at the foot of the great altar.* Above: *Dracula finds her suicide letter, stained with blood.*

15

Scholarly research has determined that the Dracula used by Bram Stoker as the model for his vampire was a real 15th-century Wallachian prince, famed for his military exploits against the Turks and for the cruel punishments he inflicted on both enemies and compatriots. The Romanian designation "Tepes" means "the impaler," referring to his favorite form of torture.

Dracula was born around 1430 on the Transylvanian plateau in north-central Romania, in the fortified town of Schassburg. Though he is linked with Transylvania and in his youth traveled still farther north to the Germanies, the realm where he reigned was the southern Romanian principality of Wallachia, bordering the Danube. His father, Vlad II (called Dracul, or "devil") was invested by the Holy Roman Emperor with the Order of the Dragon—an honor that bound its recipient to fight the infidels—and on the same occasion made Prince of Wallachia, a frontier where the Turks constantly threatened.

Vlad Tepes inherited his father's mission, carrying on a tenacious, heroic resistance against the invader over the course of three reigns spanning 1448-76, interrupted by periods of exile and imprisonment. Dracula's youthful experience of slavery in Turkey taught him the enemy's language, cunning, and political cyni-

One of only three known portraits of Dracula, this copy of an anonymous, lost original was painted in the late 16th century and hangs at Castle Ambras, near Innsbruck, Austria.

Seventeenth-century engraving of Brasov (Cronstad in German), one of the Transylvanian cities terrorized by Dracula. (Library of the Academy of Romania, Bucharest)

cism; gave him a taste for the harem; and shaped his chief character traits: suspicion and vengefulness.

As a ruler, Dracula formed short-lived alliances, employed the guerrilla tactics of his mountain-dwelling people to harass the Turks, and used terror to intimidate the sultan's forces, rebellious *boyar* nobles, and ordinary citizens. The catalog of his cruelties included not just impalement but dismembering, blinding, skinning, castrating, and sexually maiming his victims, boiling them alive and exposing them to wild animals. Even in a brutal time, his bloodthirstiness was extreme—if perhaps exaggerated by German-authored pamphlets of the day. In Romanian peasant folklore, though, he has another side: the brave warrior defending his native soil, ruthless toward the rich but a powerful friend to the poor.

Dracula was twice married, his first wife an apparent suicide. Little is known of her, but screenwriter Hart used the story as the basis for Dracula's transformation into a vampire. *In Search of Dracula*, by Raymond McNally and Radu Florescu, notes that: "According to Eastern Orthodox belief

[Dracula's church], the body of anyone bound by a curse will not be received by the earth. . . . those who die under ban of excommunication are doomed to remain 'incorrupt and entire.' . . . All this goes a long way toward explaining why vampirism has been so credible in Orthodox countries."

Bram Stoker, planning to write a vampire story and seeking an authentic background, learned about the bloody 15th-century prince from a Hungarian scholar. The results of Stoker's considerable research enrich the novel, but he erred in locating Dracula's castle on the northern reaches of Transylvania, near the Borgo Pass.

Authors McNally and Florescu led several expeditions that pinpointed the most likely site: a crumbling ruin on a Carpathian pinnacle above the river Arges in Wallachia, 140 miles south. They speculate that it was built with stones from another nearby castle often linked with Dracula, laboriously transported and laid by an unfortunate group of *boyars* whom he lured to a wedding party and then made captive. Wallachian chronicles and popular folklore also place the castle in this remote, virtually impregnable spot.

Vlad Tepes died in battle outside the city of Bucharest in 1476, at age 45. Accounts of how it happened vary, but all agree that he was decapitated and his head sent to the sultan at Constantinople as proof that their fearsome foe Kaziklu Bey (the Impaler) was no more. The rest of the historical Dracula is buried (presumably!) at the Monastery of Snagov near Bucharest. Peasants claim to have seen his ghost rising from a neighboring lake—but it is thanks to Bram Stoker that Dracula lives on around the world.

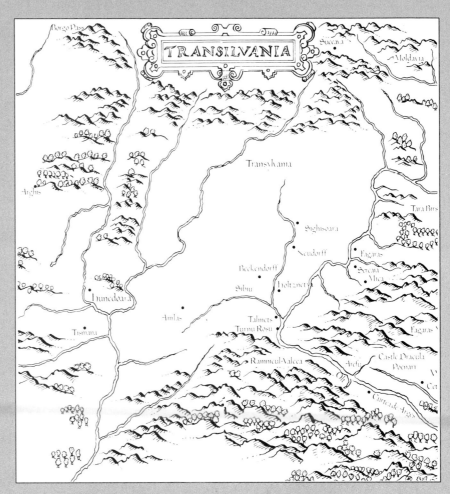

Map of Transylvania and Wallachia, from In Search of Dracula.

Turkish warrior, from The Annotated Dracula.

17

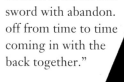

THE MAN-BEAST

Costume designer Eiko Ishioka had the challenge of giving Dracula no fewer than six different looks over the course of the film, reflecting his vastly varying age and his shape-shifting abilities. "The basic color scheme for Dracula was red, white, black, and gold," she says. "Every costume was designed to be totally unique and never seen before, to cause a fresh sensation each time Dracula appeared."

As Prince of Transylvania, Dracula is "a military genius, the incarnation of a wolf. He has the power to control all beasts. So his armor had to be quite extraordinary. I wanted to depict him in his armor as a cross between man and beast, and came up with the stylized muscle armor, like that in anatomy books. The helmet is also stylized muscles, but the effect here is a mixture of a wolf's head and a human skull. Red, the color signifying blood, is used only for Dracula, with one exception."

Gary Oldman's first fitting in the final muscle armor was the day they were to shoot the scene in the chapel, so no one knew how it would hold up under the stress of action. He refused to let the suit "wear him," lunging and swinging his sword with abandon. Predictably, pieces would fly off from time to time during takes. "They kept coming in with the soldering iron and welding me back together."

kissing, caressing, willing her back to life. He sees a bloodstained parchment in her hand.

High angle
We see Dracula's red reflection in the pool of blood and water. His hand picks up the parchment.

Low angle—from Dracula's POV
Chesare, an older monk, approaches with two other monks.

CHESARE
(Roumanian)
A message—on the shaft of a Turkish arrow—reported you killed. . . .We could not stop her. . . . Her last words . . .

Close shot
On the parchment we see superimposed what happened: Elizabeth throws herself off the castle into the river.

VOICE OF ELIZABETH
(Roumanian)
"My Prince is dead. All is lost without him. May God unite us in heaven. . ."
We pan up to closeup on Dracula reacting to the message.

Dracula's POV—low angle on Chesare

CHESARE
(Roumanian)
She has taken her own life, my son.

Closeup Elizabeth
As Chesare speaks, we track in on her and see the black shadow of the cross darkening her face.

CHESARE (O.S.)
(Roumanian)
Her soul cannot be saved. She is damned. It is God's law. . . .

Medium shot—Dracula
He cries out—a dying animal. Camera flies back to high angle, looking down, as he dumps the font of holy water, washing Elizabeth's blood across the floor.

DRACULA
(Roumanian)
Is this my reward for defending God's church?!

Low angle tracking shot

in front of Dracula as he approaches the monks.

Tracking shot over Dracula on Chesare.
Chesare moving back, raising his crucifix.

CHESARE
(Roumanian)
Sacrilege! Do not turn your back on Christ! He has chosen you to punish injustice!

Closeup low angle—Dracula

DRACULA
(Roumanian)
I renounce God—and all you hypocrites who feed off him. If my beloved burns in hell—so shall I!
(proud, powerful)
I, Dracula, Voivode of Transylvania, will arise from my own death to avenge hers with all the powers of darkness.

Low angle—medium wide
on Chesare, monks in the background. Chesare cries out. The monks wail in horror.

Dracula enters shot, grabs Chesare's wrist.

Close shot
Dracula bends Chesare's wrist in his powerful grip, snapping bones—we pan with the crucifix falling to the bloody floor.

Low angle
Dracula pushes Chesare to the ground. We see the cross above the altar.

High angle over cross
Dracula rushes and impales the cross with his sword. The chapel darkens and winds blow.

Low angle
He rakes the sacramental communion goblet through the bloody holy water—raising the cup high.

DRACULA
(Roumanian)
"The blood is the life." And it shall be mine!

He drinks from the goblet.

Anthony Hopkins in his cameo role as Chesare. Francis Coppola remarks in his production journal: "I like very much the sense that the Prologue is told through mosaic and religious icons. . . . Show the degree of Dracula's blasphemy by the reactions of these holy men."

[Dr. Van Helsing told us:] "I have asked my friend Arminius, of Buda-Pesth University, to make his record; and, from all the means that are, he tells me of what he has been. He must, indeed, have been that Voivode Dracula who won his name against the Turk, over the great river on the very frontier of Turkey-land. If it be so, then he was no common man; for in that time, and for centuries after, he was spoken of as the cleverest and most cunning, as well as the bravest of the sons of the 'land beyond the forest.' That mighty brain and that iron resolution went with him to his grave and are even now arrayed against us. The Draculas were, says Arminius, a great and noble race, though now and again were scions who were held by their coevals to have had dealings with the Evil One. . . . and in one manuscript this very Dracula is spoken of as 'wampyr'. . . ."

Right: *Storyboard art of Dracula impaling the cross.* Opposite: *A sacramental text and the set for the Transylvania convent where Jonathan Harker recovers from his visit to Castle Dracula.*

Close shot—lance in the cross
The cross starts bleeding. (Music in.)

Closeup Dracula
He looks up to the cross. Blood spattering on his face.

Wide shot
The chapel. A torrent of blood running down the steps, flowing from the impaled cross.

Closeup
On one of the stone angels in the wall; its eyes weep blood tears.

Closeup Elizabeth
on the steps. Blood around her, flooding the frame. Camera slowly drops down to close profile shot of Elizabeth. Her face sinks into the blood. Camera moves into the blood and we begin to see the microscopic view of the living cells.

Dissolve to:
[Library]

Closeup
A large, leather-bound volume lies on a reading stand. Camera pulls back as Van Helsing's hands open it. He begins to read:

High angle on Van Helsing's back
as he reads; then cut to front closeup and track in closer.

"Dracula's beloved princess was denied holy burial by the church. Damned, her soul was allowed no peace.

"Now I have searched the ancient manuscripts, the philosophies and metaphysics, devoting my life to understanding the strange things that I will relate. How these papers and journals have been placed in sequence will be made clear in the reading of them.

"Here occurs the shocking and frightening history of the wild berserker Prince Dracula. How he impaled people and roasted them and boiled their heads in a kettle. . . . How he skinned them alive and drank their blood—until, four hundred years later, he sent to far-off England for a solicitor, Mr. R. M. Renfield, to arrange for him to buy property in London.

"When Mr. Renfield returned to London, he had gone mad."

Act I

A Storm from the East

Insert:
Carfax sign, followed by Renfield's identity card

[London—Carfax Asylum]

SEWARD (V.O.)
"Medical journal of Dr. Jack Seward, Director of Carfax Asylum, London. R. M. Renfield, successful solicitor in the firm of Hawkins and Thompkins, returns from business abroad in Transylvania . . ."

Medium wide shot
Seward crosses open area of asylum, past inmates in cells, keepers going about their business. He makes notes in a small book.

SEWARD (V.O. CONTINUED)
". . . promptly suffers a complete mental breakdown, is now obsessed with some

bloodlust, and with an insatiable hunger for life in any form."

He approaches Renfield's cell.

High wide shot—through spiderweb
We see Renfield, his back to us, backlit against window of an asylum cell.

On door
Seward enters, covering his face with a handkerchief at the odor.

Low angle—Renfield
He turns and comes toward camera, and at the same time we move in on him, coming in closer and closer. Renfield turns to Seward, holding a plate of bugs and spiders. He wears thick glasses.

RENFIELD
Hors d'oeuvres, Dr. Seward? Canapés?

Closeup spider (macro)
Magnified by Renfield's lenses.

Angle on Seward
Renfield enters into two-shot, stepping behind him, reading his notes.

SEWARD
No thank you, Mr. Renfield. How are you feeling tonight?

RENFIELD
(craning to read Seward's journal)
Far better than you, my lovesick Doctor.

SEWARD
Is my personal life of interest to you?

Closeup Renfield

Mr. Renfield's credentials, one of hundreds of period documents and props created for the film.

RENFIELD
All life interests me.

Closeup blowfly
We pan with it to Renfield's mouth, and he eats it.

Closeup Seward
His reaction.

SEWARD
Your diet, Mr. Renfield, is disgusting.

On Renfield
He walks back to the window.

RENFIELD
Perfectly nutritious. Each life I ingest—gives back life to me.

SEWARD
A fly gives you life?

Through web
on Renfield.

RENFIELD
The fly's sapphire wings are typical of the aerial powers of the psychic faculties. The ancients did well when they typified the soul of a man as a butterfly!

SEWARD
(impressed)
I shall have to invent a new classification of lunatic for you.

He moves toward Renfield.

SEWARD
What about spiders? The spiders eat the flies. . . .

On Renfield
He looks up as a small bird darts across the cell.

SEWARD
What about sparrows?

RENFIELD
(becoming increasingly excited)
Did you say sparrows . . .

SEWARD
Something larger, perhaps?

On Renfield past Seward

Dr. Seward "is only nine-and-twenty, and he has an immense lunatic asylum all under his own care."

25

Renfield loses his composure, begging on Seward like a dog—

RENFIELD
A kitten, a nice little, sleek, playful kitten, that I can teach and feed and feed—no one would refuse me a kitten. I implore you—

On Seward over Renfield

SEWARD
(baiting him)
Wouldn't you prefer a cat?

RENFIELD
Yes! Yes—a cat! A big cat! My salvation depends upon it!

SEWARD
Your salvation?

RENFIELD
Lives—I need lives for the Master.

SEWARD
Master? What Master?

On Renfield over Seward
He turns and points toward the window.

RENFIELD
The Master will come! He has promised to make me immortal!

SEWARD
How?

Renfield rushes Seward, grabbing him by the throat.

Keepers enter
We pan with them as they wrestle Renfield to the ground, beating him down with clubs. He fights like an animal, snapping a keeper's wrist like a chicken bone.

RENFIELD
The blood is the life. . . .*The blood is the life!*

Close shot—Renfield
He falls to the ground, his glasses a few inches from his face.

Close shot
We see a great spider in one of the lenses. Renfield snatches it up and devours it.

Cut to:
[Hillingham Estate—garden—day]

Medium wide shot
We see the terrace and facade of Hillingham in the background. Peacocks roam, screeching mating cries. We move into two-shot of Mina Murray and Jonathan Harker, conversing under narrative spoken by Van Helsing:

Left: *Keepers pull the raving Renfield off Seward.* Overleaf: *Mina Murray and Jonathan Harker say goodbye in the garden at Hillingham.*

VAN HELSING (V.O.)
The firm regretfully sent Mr. Renfield's young assistant, Mr. Jonathan Harker, to complete the transactions. This ambitious junior clerk speedily bid adieu to his fiancée, Miss Wilhelmina Murray, and left by train on the journey to Transylvania.

MINA
You're leaving?

Two-shot 50/50—traveling in front of them

HARKER
Some foreign Count is acquiring property around London, and I am being sent to close the transactions. Money is no object. Can you imagine the power that sort of wealth commands? Think of it, Mina, royalty!

MINA
I'm thinking about our wedding, Jon.

HARKER
We can be married when I return—a grand expensive one, that Lucy and all her aristocratic friends will talk about.

He kisses her hand.

MINA
Jonathan, you know that means nothing to me. I just want us to be happy, don't you see?

HARKER
I know what's best—for both of us.

MINA
Of course. We've waited this long . . . haven't we?

HARKER
(kisses her chastely)
There is not another woman on earth can hold a wick to you!
(checking his watch, obsessed)
I must dash. I'll write—

We track back and zoom in. Mina kisses him like never before—aroused—desperate. He holds back prudishly.

MINA
Jonathan . . . I love you . . .

HARKER
I love you, my darling.

She kisses him again, seductively luring him out of frame. We are left with the peacocks. We move in on one; the eye of its feather becomes:

Right: *Storyboard art depicting Harker's train journey into Transylvania.* Below: *Prop letter from Dracula to Harker.*

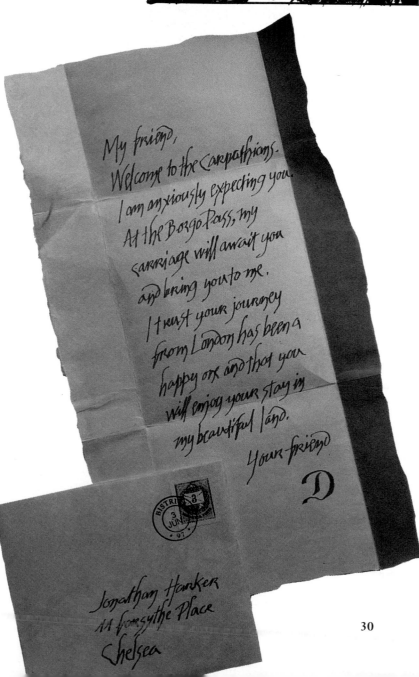

My friend,

Welcome to the Carpathians. I am anxiously expecting you. At the Borgo Pass, my carriage will await you and bring you to me. I trust your journey from London has been a happy one and that you will enjoy your stay in my beautiful land.

Your friend

D

Jonathan Harker
44 Forsythe Place
Chelsea

[Train tunnel—day]

Dark, a light at the end. Camera moves toward the red sun. (Music cue: sounds of the rails.)

Superimpose:
Mina's portrait, which fades into Harker's face in closeup.

[Orient Express—sunset]

Wide shot
The train moves across the top of the frame, traveling downward. Superimposed over the lower part of the frame we see Harker's journal:

HARKER (V.O.)
"25th May. Six days out of London. Left Buda-Pesth early this morning. The impression I had was that we were leaving the West and entering the East. . . ."

Superimpose: medium closeup
Harker at the train window.

Superimpose: low angle—rails moving past strange countryside.

[Transylvania frontier—sunset]

Wide shot
The train travels down through the magnificent Carpathian Mountains, taking us into the heart of Transylvanian darkness.

HARKER (V.O.)
"The district I am to enter is in the extreme east of the country, just on the borders of three states, Transylvania, Moldavia, and Bukovina, in the midst of the Carpathian Mountains. . . ."

Superimpose insert: map of Eastern Europe
We notice the region of "Transylvania."

HARKER (V.O., CONTINUED)
". . . one of the wildest and least known portions of Europe. I was not able to light on any map giving the exact locality of Castle Dracula. Mem., I acknowledge receipt of the letter dated 18 May from the Count."

[Interior of Orient Express—sunset]

Close on Harker
(Music cue.) The map dissolves away.

Descending into the landscape
The clouds outside dissolve into Dracula's eyes.

DRACULA
"My Friend, Welcome to the Carpathians. I am anxiously expecting you. . . ."

Harker in the foreground becomes darkened by shadow. We see only the eyes.

Superimpose: Dracula's letter
in purple ink—elegant handwriting from another age.

DRACULA
"At the Borgo Pass, my carriage will await you and bring you to me. I trust your journey from London has been a happy one and that you will enjoy your stay in my beautiful land. Your friend, D."

Camera moves close on the "D." Music in.

[Coach—night]

Medium wide shot
A coach traveling downward through the Carpathian mountains.

Cut to interior, view on passengers in turn: Harker, nervously checking his watch; a bearded, bespectacled merchant; two gypsy peasant women (one old, one young). The old woman leans forward suddenly and stabs a strange two-fingered sign at Harker. Outside, lightning strikes in the shape of the sign.

The gypsy woman made "that strange mixture of fear-meaning movements which I had seen outside the hotel at Bistritz—the sign of the cross and the guard against the evil eye."

[Borgo Road—continuing action]

Wide shot

The coach stops by a clearing, in which stands a grotesque shrine bearing a wolf's head with bared fangs. The road sign indicates the way to the next town. Leery about waiting here too long, the driver starts taking down Harker's baggage.

HARKER
We are early. No one is here.

Medium closeup—gypsy girl

The young gypsy woman folds her crucifix into his hand.

GYPSY GIRL
(Roumanian)
The dead travel fast.

Closeup Harker

looking at the crucifix in his hand.

Reverse wide shot

The Slovak driver opens the door, points the way.

[Clearing—night]

Wide shot

Harker steps out, protesting. The driver makes no delay in continuing on his way. Harker is left alone in this desolate spot. He looks up.

His POV—the wolf-head shrine

We hear the wolves.

Closeup Harker

He stands alone, fearful.

High angle

Wolves looking down at Harker.

New angle

32

Suddenly, out of the mist black stallions appear, pulling a caleche coach with a black skirt over the wheels. We pan with the coach. Lantern rays fall across the Dark Driver reining in the stallions. He leans down to Harker.

DARK DRIVER
My Master the Count bade me take all good care of you, mein Herr.

Medium shot Harker
Before he can respond, he is lifted into the caleche. View shifts to interior as Harker lands in the caleche, petrified, hearing his luggage being loaded. We see his reaction in closeup as the caleche pulls away.

Wide shot—behind caleche
The caleche leaves.

[Caleche interior—traveling—night]
Medium shot Harker
The caleche moving. The partition in the ceiling suddenly snaps back, startling him. A hand holding a flask of plum brandy comes in. Harker takes it. The partition closes abruptly.

Harker looks out the window to the driver.

HARKER
I say, is the castle far? Is it far to the castle?

The driver, seated much too far away to have passed him the brandy, ignores him. Wolves howl. More of them. Closer.

Back to Harker
We track in close to him; he freezes, looking out the window.

[Borgo Road—traveling—night]

Close shot—a wheel
almost going off the edge for a moment.

Harker's POV—high angle looking down
We see the caleche going dangerously close to the edge of the abyss. We see the river two hundred feet below.

Francis Coppola notes: "The high point of this sequence is when Harker is picked up by the ghostly coach. The Dark Driver should be an Ichabod Crane image, extremely frightening. We don't see his face clearly, only his hat and his body and his enormous strength."

Jonathan Harker's Journal

Suddenly, away on our left, I saw a faint flickering blue flame. The driver saw it at the same moment; he at once checked the horses and, jumping to the ground, disappeared into the darkness. I did not know what to do, the less as the howling of the wolves grew closer; but while I wondered the driver suddenly appeared again, and without a word took his seat, and we resumed our journey. I think I must have fallen asleep and kept dreaming of the incident, for it seemed to be repeated endlessly, and now looking back, it is like a sort of awful nightmare. . . . Once there appeared a strange optical effect: when [the driver] stood between me and the flame he did not obstruct it, for I could see its ghostly flicker all the same.

[Later] He—the Count—explained to me that it was commonly believed that on a certain night of the year—last night, in fact, when all evil spirits are supposed to have unchecked sway—a blue flame is seen over any place where treasure has been concealed.

Roman Coppola on the blue flame:

"The blue flame was an optical effect, not one of the old techniques—but the shape of the flame itself we borrowed from F. W. Murnau's *Faust*."

Francis Coppola:

"Historically the blue flame represents the treasures of Dracula, but we'll use it a little differently . . . to suggest his power, almost as if it was Dracula's forcefield."

Multiple exposure:
Scores of wolves eyes gleam in the darkness. One set of eyes dissolves to:

Side angle
The Dark Driver.

Cut to:
[Castle Dracula—exterior]

Wide shot from below
Camera pans around crumbling walls.

Over horses
Suddenly a strange blue flame floats in the darkness ahead—horses spook and whinny. The stallions wheel and sweep the caleche away through the blue flames toward the castle. Harker looks at the crucifix, opens his coat.

Dissolve to:
[Courtyard—night]

Wide low angle
The caleche approaches and drives through the tunnel into the courtyard.

Caleche window—camera looking back
Harker sticks his head out window, looks forward, turns, and sees successive tunnel gates closing behind him.

[Inner courtyard—night]

Medium low angle
The caleche enters frame. The Dark Driver sets a frightened Harker down, then his luggage, and drives away.

High wide overhead angle
looking down at the courtyard. The stone castle appears a vast ruin. Sections of the walls and foundation have tumbled down and are resting on the ground. Harker, small, looks around. A rock falls, startling him. He starts to climb the steps, carrying his luggage.

On Harker's back
walking up the stairs, approaching the door. We see his shadow move up the wall. The door opens.

Harker—head on
He walks into a medium closeup.

His POV
The terrifying shadow of a monster, turning to him, hands menacing.

Jonathan Harker, the solicitor's clerk who travels to Transylvania to close some real estate deals and thus sets the plot of *Dracula* in motion, is played in the film by young American star Keanu Reeves. According to Reeves, the character of Harker is "modeled on the Victorian gentleman ideal. He's a very conservative man, a family man, a man with a life plan. He's been working hard since he was sixteen."

Harker starts out as a young man very concerned with making his mark in life—ambitious, class-conscious, a bit of a prude. "He's obsessed with time," screenwriter Jim Hart notes. The very first line of Stoker's novel is an entry in Harker's journal reading "Left Munich at 8:35 p.m. on 1st May; should have arrived [at Vienna] early next morning at 6:46 but train was a hour late." He even checks his watch as his fiancée, Mina Murray, is kissing him goodbye.

But Harker takes a life-changing journey in the course of the story: terrorized by his Transylvanian host, raped by the vampire Brides, escaping by almost superhuman courage, witnessing his beloved sharing blood with the arch-fiend Dracula, and hunting the vampire prince to his final grave. "In the beginning he's a hero and by the end he's a shadow of what he was," says Francis Coppola—a transformation represented by Harker's hair turning white. It is a less arrogant but wiser man who reclaims his bride at the close.

Of the director, Reeves says, "What he wants is an odyssey from each person, and he'll do anything to make that real. He'll give you experiences to build stories upon. He wants you to go off on your journey, to be involved."

Reeves most recently appeared as the young street hustler in Gus Van Sant's *My Own Private Idaho*, and in 1991 co-starred with Patrick Swayze in *Point Break*. He is also known for his role in the comedy *Bill and Ted's Excellent Adventure* and its sequel.

Raised in Toronto, Reeves performed in local theater productions and on television before beginning his film career. He gained notice in Tim Hunter's *River's Edge*, and his other notable roles include the young chevalier in Stephen Frears' *Dangerous Liaisons* as well as parts in *Parenthood* and *I Love You to Death*.

Did he enjoy playing Jonathan Harker? "He's an earnest, humble, pure man. He's fun to play. And I'm working with some of the best actors around. It was an amazing part to be offered, and I've had some of the best days of my life on this film."

Back to Harker
His reaction.

[Castle doorway—night]

Harker's POV—the same shadow
View pans, revealing what created the shadow: Dracula, a tall old man. Hands long and hairy. Face riveting, handsome like a Tartar—and horrible at the same time. His eyes a cold, vivid blue. He puts down a bowl of fruit and an Oriental lantern (that made shadow grotesque) for his guest. He stands there like a statue. We pull back to include Harker.

DRACULA
Welcome to my house. Enter freely of your own will—and leave some of the happiness you bring!

HARKER
Count . . . Dracula?

DRACULA
(smiling, courtly bow)
I am Dracula, and I bid you welcome, Mr. Harker, to my house. Come in—the night air is chill, and you must need to eat and rest.

Close shot—at the threshold (reverse action)
Harker enters "freely," taking that fateful step across the threshold. Dracula turns and leads him into the castle. The great door closes with a boom.

[Castle hallway—night]

Following sequence is tracking projection with Harker (on the plate) following Dracula, who carries his bags. As they walk, the lantern casts bizarre moving shadows. Dracula moves oddly through the corridors; Harker follows.

DRACULA
Come, tell me of the properties you have procured for me.

HARKER
The most remarkable is Carfax Estate. The house there is quite large and of all periods, back, I should say, to medieval times.

They step up a spiral staircase. Harker is overwhelmed by the Greek and Roman statues in perfect condition lining the stairs. The walls are filled with a fortune in primitive museum-caliber weapons. Full suits of armor stand about.

DRACULA
A house cannot be made habitable in a day; and after all, how few days go to make up a century.

Dracula exits offstage, Harker following— but then Dracula appears behind him, leading him another way.

DRACULA
I come from an old family, and to live in a new house would kill me.

High-angle wide shot
A ruin of a battlement protrudes in the center of the mosaic floor. A huge block of stone has crumbled to the floor. We see the mosaic of a huge cross on the floor, broken and pitted. Dracula and Harker walk across it. (Music out.)

[Great Hall—night]

Wide shot
Harker is seated at a large table set with a sumptuous meal for one. A fireplace in the background. Grand masterworks of European art and medieval tapestries punctuate the elegance and impeccable taste of the appointments.

DRACULA
You will, I trust, excuse me that I do not join you, but I have already dined and I never drink . . . wine.

He pours wine for Harker.

Eiko Ishioka on Dracula's crest:

"For Dracula's crest, I designed a motif of several elements—dragon, wolf, snakes, birds, and fire—intertwined in a single form. It appears throughout the film, in costumes, sets, and props, as a symbol of Dracula."

Francis Coppola adds:

"When Dracula first meets Harker, he tells him a little family history. About the Order of the Dragon. 'Dracul' means devil and also dragon. That's the name of Dracula's father, who was inducted into this society dedicated to fighting Turks and heretics. Dracula starts out as a dragon slayer, like St. George; then he becomes the dragon."

THE AMBIGUOUS HOST

When Jonathan Harker is welcomed by the old Dracula, in his sweeping scarlet cloak and startling Kabuki hair, costume designer Eiko "chose to emphasize the androgynous quality in his character.

"I wanted to give Dracula an infinite variety of personality," she says, "so that his true self is not easily revealed, remaining a mystery to the audience. Is he a man or a beast? Devil or angel? Male or female? He is is constantly changing, in a different mood each time, like a kaleidoscope."

From Francis Coppola's notes for this scene: "Here's where we really introduce the world of Dracula, and we ought to feel as though we're coming into his world . . . with that Byzantine, oriental feel to it."

Eiko continues: "In his youth Dracula lived in Istanbul and would have been influenced by Turkish culture and dress, as seen in this costume. Embroidered on the breast is Dracula's crest or emblem. The cloak is red, the color symbolizing Dracula. The enormous train was designed to undulate, when he rushes about his castle, like a sea of blood."

Eiko collaborated with makeup/hair designer Michele Burke-Winter to invent the unique hairstyle; the 400-year-old face was the creation of special makeup designer Greg Cannom. The overall effect of costume, hair, and makeup aimed for and conveyed "a haunting asexuality."

Medium closeup—Harker

HARKER
This chalice is Persian—is it not? Exquisite piece, Count. Worthy of kings.

Low angle—past Harker to Dracula
He steps back and leans against a wall, studying Harker.

Back to Harker
He looks around the room, marveling, and notices an old painting:

His POV—the painting
The young warrior Dracula, wearing the royal insignia.

HARKER
An ancestor? I see the resemblance.

Medium shot—Dracula

DRACULA
The Order of Dracul, the dragon. An ancient society pledging my forefathers to defend the church against all enemies of Christ.

(mirthless smile)
Alas, the relationship was not entirely . . . successful.

Harker laughs uneasily, trying to be polite. Dracula draws a massive sword, slashing it about, terrifying Harker.

DRACULA
It is no laughing matter! We Draculs have a right to be proud! What devil or witch was ever so great as Attila, whose blood flows in these veins!

Dracula entertains Harker on his arrival. The statuary arm holding the torch is Coppola's homage to Jean Cocteau's Beauty and the Beast.

Dracula enters into two-shot. He bows, accepting the apology.

DRACULA
Forgive me, *my* young friend. I am not accustomed to . . . guests. And my heart is weary with many years of mourning over the dead.

Dissolve to:
[Great Hall—night—later]

Close shot
Dracula's white hand, the long nails filed to clawlike points, Oriental fashion.

Superimpose multiple images of:
A big pot of royal ink. An ornate signature, "Voivodul Vlad Draculea" on a deed of purchase. An image of Carfax.

DRACULA (O.S.)
I do so long to go through the crowded streets of your mighty London, to be in the midst of the whirl and rush of humanity—to share its life, its changes, its death. . . .

Low angle
Dracula stands on the left side of table, his back to the fireplace; we see Harker seated. We see Dracula's map of London on the wall behind Harker, Dracula's shadow on the map. Dracula moves to the map, and we track with him over the table. Harker places the hot waxen seal on the deed.

HARKER
There. You, Count, are the owner of Carfax Abbey at Purfleet. Congratulations.

He turns to Dracula—Dracula is gone, but his shadow on the map changes grotesquely. We pan with Harker as he turns and sees: Dracula—on the other side of him. Harker turns (view over his shoulder on Dracula) and extends his hand to shake. Dracula opens both hands and bows.

Gary Oldman says, exaggerating slightly, "I think there is one closeup in this film and it is on my silky palms."

Back to Harker
His frightened reaction.

Wider on Dracula
Drained—saddened—

DRACULA
Blood is too precious a thing in these times.

He draws the sword across his own palm, drawing blood. He stares at it, tempted, then closes his fist.

DRACULA (CONTINUES)
The warlike days are over. The victories of my great race are but a tale to be told . . . I am the last of my kind.

On Harker
He stands. Camera tilts up.

HARKER
I have offended you with my ignorance, Count. Forgive me.

Voivodul Vlad Draculea

40

Closeup Harker
He masks his reaction.

Close shot
Dracula's hands. Silken hair lines his palms.

Medium closeup Dracula
We pan him to the map of London, marked with a red circle.

Close shot—the map
Carfax Abbey; includes a photo of Renfield, as agent.

DRACULA
Your firm writes most highly of your talents, that you are a man of good . . . taste.
(enjoying private joke)
They say you are a "worthy substitute" to your predecessor, Mr. Renfield. . . .

Dracula's POV—over Harker
organizing the photoplates on the great table.

HARKER
(seizing the praise)
Yes, I've replaced Mr. Renfield in all matters. Forgive my curiosity—but Carfax Abbey, the property you have chosen, is a ruin. It would require renovation before it would be suitable for you. Do you plan to go to London soon, Count?

Harker turns to the map (moving out of frame right). We track in slowly on the table, and see the shadow of Dracula's hand suddenly spill the ink. We track in, seeing the bloodlike ink spreading near the photoplate of Mina.

Medium closeup Dracula
We track in slowly on Dracula, riveted to the photoplate—so still he looks dead.

DRACULA
(passionate whisper)
Very wise, my young friend. Do you believe in destiny?

Close shot—Mina's photoplate
Somewhat inkstained. Dracula's wolflike hand clutching it.

Two-shot—Dracula and Harker
Dracula in foreground staring at the photoplate, Harker in background.

Above: *Dracula's giant map of London was projected on the castle wall.* Left: *Framed daguerrotype of Mina.*

41

The Castle Dracula set under construction, showing 19th-century ironwork propping up the stone ruins.

Coppola's *Dracula* was shot entirely on sound stages rather than locations, for both budgetary and stylistic reasons. "The decision opened up the possibility that the approach could be a little adventurous," Coppola says. "We could control the settings in an artistic and unusual and beautiful way."

Early on, Coppola seriously considered the radical approach of shooting the film with backdrops of black curtains, scrims, and projections—believing that the extraordinary costumes should set the mood. Even after this idea was modified in favor of more conventional sets, the director emphasized that he didn't want "hard sets that imitate reality"—the standard for costume dramas. He was seeking a more poetic and emotional depiction of the story's environments and especially "a highly imaginative use of space and shadow." A key concept was the "black limbo"—areas of deep shadow behind the lighted parts of the set, suggesting the infinite distance behind the undead Dracula.

Production designer Tom Sanders faced formidable challenges. In *Dracula*, his first assignment as PD, he had to realize the creative vision of a renowned filmmaker. And because an earlier set of designs hadn't satisfied the the director, he

Production designer Tom Sanders with one of his models.

got off to a late start—his crew was still designing and building sets during principal photography. "We started with a clean slate," Sanders says. "He gave us the general directions to make it look like any other Dracula movie—and to make it strange. We also worked off Francis's storyboards and some of the Symbolist paintings."

Sanders had just finished working on Stephen Spielberg's *Hook* when he returned to Sony Studios (the legendary former MGM lot) to begin *Dracula*—in fact, the *Hook* sets were being struck to make room for his new creations. They had 58 sets to construct on six different stages. "We didn't have time to do a lot of preliminary drawings," he says. "So I made fully executed models of all the sets, and these were used as a visual guide throughout the process."

Sanders credits his crew of up to 150 artisans for making it all come together. "We had carpenters, plasterers, a sculpting crew, modelmakers, greensmen—it's a collaboration among all these crafts, and every one

of these guys is responsible for pulling something off. On this movie we turned over each stage three or four times. We'd just get through building something and at the same time be designing another set to take its place."

Castle Dracula was perhaps the most important creation, and Coppola had some strong ideas about this set. "What if Dracula's castle is partly ruined—if parts of it had crumbled and were shored up with some more modern structure? Maybe Dracula, who was in touch with the scientific innovations of his day, hired someone like Gustave Eiffel to prop up his castle with steel?" That idea was translated into the striking exterior of the filmed castle.

Sanders notes: "In the real world, in Hillingham, we've kept the elements pretty realistic, but whenever we got into anything to do with Dracula, we twisted the architecture, so that the minute you walked in the door of Dracula's castle, you'd be lost. It's another dimension in there."

The Chapel, where much of the Prologue takes place, was really two sets. Its 1462 incarnation was built on a high platform and in pristine condition. When the story resumes 400 years later, it is reconstructed on the main stage level as a swampy netherworld of impaled victims, its

crumbling walls trussed by steel girders, its sculpture blackened by time.

Like all the key people on the film, Sanders benefited from Coppola's experimental bent. "Francis encouraged us to try different things. He said from the beginning, don't worry about looking bad—if anyone's going to look bad, it's going to be me." Once the director even stopped by Sanders's office with a book of Japanese origami and asked him: "Can we make sets like this?"

Production drawing of the castle tower, later rendered as a matte painting.

The Symbolist painting Resistance—The Black Idol, *by Frantisek Kupka, one of the design team's models for the castle exterior. (Prague, Narodní Gallery)*

Mina Murray at her typewriter.

DRACULA
(continues)
That even the powers of time can be altered for a single purpose—
(pause)
The luckiest man who walks on this earth is the one who finds—true love.

He turns away, hiding his orgasmic reaction. Harker comes back to the table.

HARKER
(embarrassed, checking his pocket)
Ah—you found—Mina. I thought she was lost. We're to be married as soon as I return.

Camera pulls back and we see Dracula's shadow growing and moving as if to strangle Harker. We hear a rustle of feminine garments and laughter. Harker looks around—nothing. Dracula doesn't react.

HARKER
(continues)
Are you married? Count—sir—are you married?

Closeup Dracula
Harker in the background.

DRACULA
I was married . . . ages ago it seems. She died. . . .

HARKER
I'm very sorry.

DRACULA
She was fortunate. My life at its best is . . . misery.
(hands Harker the photo)
She will no doubt make a devoted wife. And you a faithful husband.

Medium wide shot (reverse)
Dracula turns, suddenly all business.

DRACULA
Write now, my friend, to your firm, and to any . . . loved ones, and say that it shall please you to stay with me until a month from now.

HARKER
(taken aback)
A month? You wish me to stay so long?

DRACULA
I desire it much. You have much to tell me of London and other interests I may wish to pursue with your . . . talents. I will take no refusal.

Dracula exits past Harker; camera moves back fast, leaving a surprised Harker alone in the room (Dracula's shadow getting bigger and bigger, and he is gone).

To black, then cut to:

[Hillingham Estate—day]

We reveal the exterior tableau of Hillingham. Superimposed over the tableau we see a diary being typed on an early typewriter.

VAN HELSING (V.O.)
Now, from the diary of Miss Wilhelmina Murray, 30th May 1897:

Dissolve to:
[Hillingham House—conservatory—day]

Wide shot
Mina sitting at a table, typing. Her back to us. Track in on her hands typing:

MINA (V.O.)
"I am staying for some weeks at Hillingham,

44

The main staircase at Hillingham.

the estate of my wealthy friend Lucy West-enra. Though I am only a schoolmistress and she an aristocrat, we have laughed and cried together since we were children, and now we dream of being married together."

Medium closeup—Mina
Her schoolmistress attire designed to prevent any sensuality from escaping. Her eyes drift to a book open beside her.

Close shot—typewriter keys
jamming. We pan to Sir Richard Burton's *Arabian Nights* open beside her as she turns the page.

MINA
Oh . . . how disgustingly awful. . . .

LUCY (O.S.)
Mina! Mina!

Lucy enters
breathless. She is twenty, spoiled, rich,

coquettish. We pan and track her to Mina.

LUCY
Oh, no! You're always working. Is your ambitious Jon Harker forcing you to learn that ridiculous machine—when he could be forcing you to perform unspeakable acts of desperate passion on the parlor floor?

Close on Mina over Lucy

MINA
Lucy, really—you shouldn't talk about my fiancé in that way. There's more to marriage than carnal pleasures—

Medium wide two-shot
Mina stands—the book falls to the floor.

LUCY
So I see . . . much much more. Show me those pictures!

The girls burst into laughter. They sit on

45

Mina and Lucy pore over the Arabian Nights.

the floor, both breathlessly fanning pages to other etchings.

Close shot—over girls
on the open book.

MINA
He's so appallingly huge—

LUCY
They come much bigger.

Back to two-shot
Lucy pantomimes with her hands. Mina is aghast.

MINA
Lucy! Oh, can a man and woman really do—
(searching for a particular picture)
that?

LUCY
I did—only last night. . . .

MINA
Fibber—you didn't.

LUCY
Yes, I did . . . in my dreams.

They laugh—Mina reflective.

LUCY
Jonathan . . . measures up, doesn't he? You can tell Lucy.

MINA
We've kissed, that's all.
(smiles)
He thinks he's too poor to marry me. He wants to buy me an expensive ring, and I try to tell him it doesn't matter. It's all the worse now that I'm visiting here at Hilling-ham . . . my "rich friend."

LUCY
(full of admiration)
Oh, Mina, you're the most splendid girl in all the world!

MINA
And you are the one with regiments of men falling at your feet. . . .

LUCY

—but not even one marriage proposal. And here I am almost twenty—practically a hag.

Fade out. Fade in:

[Hillingham—main room—evening]

Medium wide shot
A small party in progress. A harpist is playing selections from Gilbert and Sullivan. Lucy rushes up to Mina, who is standing by the window in a party dress.

LUCY
Oh, Mina, I'm so happy I don't know what to do with myself. I think I'm about to have three marriage proposals in one evening. I do hope there's enough of me to go around! Look.

The butler, Hobbs, intones the name of a guest who has just entered.

HOBBS
Mister Quincey P. Morris!

Girls' POV
Quincey Morris, a handsome young man, wide-brimmed hat in his hand, Western boots, embroidered vest flashing under his waistcoat. Hobbs tries to relieve him of his hat but the smiling Quincey won't relinquish it.

Close two-shot—girls

MINA
What is that?

LUCY
A Texan. Quincey P. Morris. He's so young and fresh—like a wild stallion between my legs.

Quincey strolls past a groaning buffet table, plucks a morsel off a tray, tosses it in the air and catches it in his mouth, to the horror or amusement of witnesses.

MINA
(laughing)
You are positively indecent.

LUCY
I just know what men desire. Watch.

Lucy rushes off to her Texan, leaving Mina watching.

ARABIAN NIGHTS IN VICTORIAN MORNING ROOMS

Garrett Lewis's set design for the Hillingham conservatory.

With the incident where Mina and Lucy excitedly peruse a volume of the *Arabian Nights*, we are immediately reminded of the Eastern flavor in Stoker's novel, its Transylvanian setting, and Victorian culture. In an early script discussion, Francis Coppola says: "So the young girls are titillated and talking about coming into their maturity . . . we'll introduce these characters in London 1897, the context of the Arabian Nights fantasies, where men were men and women and girls were slaves."

Coppola also notes in his journal that the region Dracula comes from "had many component nationalities. It was here that the expanding Ottoman Empire was interfacing with the Holy Roman Empire." Visually conveying this meeting of East and West was the responsibility of production designer Tom Sanders and especially costume designer Eiko Ishioka, who brought her own heritage and international style to the task.

The recreation of mosaics and icons from the Eastern Orthodox church; costumes whose fabrics, detailing, and colors reflected Byzantine decor; the use of furs later in the film to suggest Russian influence—all manifested this blending of cultures.

Straightlaced Victorian England was fascinated by the sensual Orient and the freedom it implied. The *Arabian Nights* and its translator, explorer-hedonist Sir Richard Burton, were subjects for scandal. Many paintings of the *fin de siècle*, "showed the Byzantine influence," as Coppola notes.

Bram Stoker met Burton in the 1880s and wrote how impressed he was "not only by Burton's accounts but also by his physical appearance—especially his canine teeth," according to *In Search of Dracula*. The *Arabian Nights* contains a vampire tale, and Burton also translated some Hindu stories involving vampires. Stoker pays homage to this role model in *Dracula*, having Jonathan Harker comment about his eerie sojourn at Castle Dracula: "This diary seems horribly like the beginning of the 'Arabian Nights,' for everything has to break off at cockcrow."

A sedate party at Hillingham, except for Lucy and Quincey flirting on a couch, at right. The designers avoided fussy Victorian mouldings and other details, using neutral sandstone walls so that the wardrobe would stand out.

Mina's POV—Lucy and Quincey

LUCY
Quincey!

QUINCEY
(kisses her hand)
Miss Lucy! Why you're as fresh as a spring rain.

LUCY
Quincey, please — let me touch it. It's so big.

Giddy, Lucy reaches for his crotch. She slowly raises his big Bowie knife into view, fondles it seductively. Then she kisses him passionately, tugging him to her bare shoulders, her breast.

View on servants
reacting, shocked.

Back to Mina
laughing at Lucy's antics.

On Lucy and Quincey
He leads her to a couch.

QUINCEY
Little girl . . . Oh, my dear sweet little girl. . . .

LUCY
Oh, Quincey, you are so very sweet and dear. . . .

On Mina
She turns to look toward the foyer.

Mina's POV—the foyer
Jack Seward entering; an intense "worka-holic" in his early thirties. He nervously cleans his nails with a surgical lancet.

HOBBS
Dr. Jack Seward!

Superimpose:
Mina's typewritten diary. (Music cue with typing.)

MINA (V.O.)
"Number Two—brilliant Jack Seward. A superb doctor, he has an immense lunatic asylum all under his own care. This should prepare him well for life with Lucy."
Pan with Seward to Lucy, who rushes to his arms.

LUCY
Jack! Oceans of love, millions of kisses.

As Seward greets Lucy, he sees Quincey. He stumbles and falls. The servants help Seward up and to the couch. Lucy fusses over him.

LUCY
My poor little doctor . . . brilliant doctor.

Seward and Quincey exchange terse greetings.

LUCY
Your pulse is all right. . . .

View on Mina
As she is watching this scene, she hears some commotion outside, turns, and looks out.

Mina's POV through window
Arthur Holmwood exits his luxurious coach. Rich, handsome, imperious. He enters the foyer.

HOBBS
Arthur Holmwood, Esquire!

MINA (V.O.)
"Number Three—Arthur Holmwood, the future Lord Godalming. It seems that Quincey, Seward, and Holmwood had adventured together around the world, and now they've all fallen in love with the same girl."

Holmwood enters; Lucy greets him. He gets a big kiss and more flirtatious chatter.

View on Quincey and Seward
seeing Holmwood. Seward sits down on Quincey's hat. Quincey takes the hat and bangs it back into shape. Lucy gestures to Mina to join them all as Holmwood greets his fellow suitors.

MINA (V.O.)
"He is everything Lucy requires in a husband. Excellent *parti*, of good birth, and dreadfully wealthy."

Wide shot party
Lucy drops one of her diamond earrings. She directs Quincey and Seward to look for it while she surreptitiously kisses Holmwood. The men crawl around the floor. Quincey comes up with the earring.

LUCY
Oh, Quincey found it! You get the reward.
(kisses him)
Now we're going to play in the garden. . . .

A grotesque shadow moves across the scene, ominous against the youth and passion of Lucy and her suitors. We pan with the shadow as it moves, turning to Mina, covering her. We see her puzzled unease.

Letter, Quincey P. Morris to Hon. Arthur Holmwood.

"25 May.

"My dear Art,—
        "We've told yarns by the camp-fire in the prairies; and dressed one another's wounds after trying a landing at the Marquesas; and drunk healths on the shore of Titicaca. There are more yarns to be told, and other wounds to be healed, and another health to be drunk. Won't you let this be at my camp-fire tomorrow night? I have no hesitation in asking you, as I know a certain lady is engaged to a certain dinner-party, and that you are free. There will only be one other, our old pal at the Korea, Jack Seward. He's coming, too, and we both want to mingle our weeps over the wine-cup, and to drink a health with all our hearts to the happiest man in all the wide world, who has won the noblest heart that God has made and the best worth winning. We promise you a hearty welcome, and a loving greeting, and a health as true as your own right hand. We shall both swear to leave you at home if you drink too deep to a certain pair of eyes. Come!

"Yours as ever and always,
        "QUINCEY P. MORRIS"

DRACULA (V.O.)
(Roumanian)
You are the love of my life. . . .

Cut to:
[Castle Dracula—exterior]

Wide shot
The front of the castle on the promontory (matte painting, etc.) The ancient castle has partially crumbled, but has been saved by steel.

Insert:
Dracula's face, with its burning eyes, emerges briefly from the shadows.

Left to right: Sadie Frost as Lucy Westenra, Richard E. Grant as Dr. Jack Seward, Cary Elwes as Arthur Holmwood, and Bill Campbell as Quincey Morris.

Bram Stoker's *Dracula* is rich in characters and plot threads that have never before found their way to the screen. Among the most notable are the three young men who share a passion for adventure and for the beautiful Lucy Westenra.

Quincey Morris, Lord Arthur Holmwood, and Dr. Jack Seward are well-off gentlemen who have grown close traveling together in exotic places; the novel refers in passing to some of their exploits. Yet they are very different: Quincey is a cattleman from Texas, an easygoing American aristocrat, while Holmwood is a slightly stuffy British peer. The somewhat older Seward— "brilliant Jack," as Lucy calls him—oversees a lunatic asylum, a career that emphasizes his thoughtful, somewhat melancholic temperament.

"All of the characters in our movie are, in their personalities and function, like the characters in the book," notes Francis Coppola. "With Quincey there's the unusual angle of a rich young American seen from the 1890s London point of view. . . . Dr. Seward is an intriguing character and never portrayed, though he's in half the book."

Seward is played by Richard E. Grant, who was most recently seen as the compromising British film director in Robert Altman's *The Player*. The South African born actor has co-starred in *L.A. Story*, *Henry and June*, and *Mountains of the Moon*, and is also known for his stage and television work in England. He says, "I think Francis's idea about Seward was that he's on the edge of madness himself—due to unrequited love and his drug addiction. The viewer should be unclear as to who is madder: the man running the asylum or the man who is in it."

Arthur Holmwood is depicted by expatriate English actor Cary Elwes, whose first major role was in *The Princess Bride*. He has performed with the Royal Shakespeare Company and co-starred in *Glory*, *Days of Thunder*, and the spoof *Hot Shots!* "Holmwood is impetuous and used to getting things his own way," Elwes says of his character, "and he's traumatized by the death of his fiancée. When his world starts crumbling around him, he has to change. He represents order, like what you see at Hillingham. But the moment Dracula arrives on the scene, he throws everything into disorder, including Holmwood's mind."

Bill Campbell as Quincey Morris comes to Dracula from his starring role in his feature film debut, *The Rocketeer*. He has guest-starred and been a series regular on several TV shows, and his stage credits include Shakesperean roles and musical comedy. After finishing work on *Dracula*, he headed back to the New York stage for a Broadway production of *Hamlet*. Coppola found in him the "natural young Texan" he was seeking for Quincey—"someone with a wonderful personality who can also do the comedy that's in there." In relation to the triumvirate, Campbell sees Quincey as "the guy who sort of holds them together. He's the guy, you know, when you were a kid, who always had the baseball bat and the glove and the ball."

The young actors all had a good time preparing for and shooting *Dracula*; during rehearsals at his home in the Napa Valley Coppola sent them off ballooning and horseback riding to bond as a unit. But there was a darker undercurrent to their roles as well. Richard E. Grant observes that "Francis has locked into the obsessive nature of all these characters. Each shows a different side of unrequited love and lust."

[Guest bedroom—night]

Split diopter shot
We see close up Harker's open journal on a writing stand. A small shadow in the shape of Castle Dracula is cast upon the page. On the right side we see in the distance Harker next to the window, in front of a basin, shaving.

HARKER (V.O)
"30th May. Castle Dracula. I doubt; I fear; I think strange things which I dare not confess to my own soul. I wish I were safe out of this place, or that I had never come. There is something uncanny about the Count. The way he looked at the picture of Mina fills me with dread; as if I have a part to play in a story that is not known to me."

Close shot—Dracula's hand
gliding to Harker, flexing in anticipation—

Close shot (trick)
Over Harker's shoulder into the mirror. We see Dracula's hand land gently on Harker's shoulder, but we don't see it in the mirror.

Closeup Harker
He turns, startled.

HARKER
I didn't hear you come in.
Harker's POV—over his shoulder

Dracula in the distance, way across the room by the door! He holds blankets, puts them on the bed. Then he moves fast (but without taking a step) into two-shot with Harker. Harker turns to the mirror, amazed he saw no one behind him.

DRACULA
Take care how you cut yourself—it is more dangerous than you think.

Close shot—mirror (trick)
The mirror magically implodes as Dracula shields his face from it.

DRACULA
A foul bauble of man's vanity. Perhaps you should . . . grow a beard.

Medium shot—over Dracula on Harker
Dracula snatches the bloody razor from Harker's hand, turns, and licks it clean with a delicate sweep across his tongue (that Harker doesn't see). He savors it erotically.

DRACULA
The letters I requested—have you written them?

Harker reluctantly hands him the letters. Dracula flips through them impatiently, lingers over the envelope bearing Mina's name.

51

A supernatural being, Dracula can move without walking, change his shape, appear and disappear at will; he does not reflect in mirrors. Stoker's novel is full of unearthly events like hovering blue flames and monsters in the form of mist. Coppola's *Dracula* sought ways to create magical special effects without the slick high-tech methods of computer animation, "morphing," and blue screen.

"We didn't have the budget to compete with the big movies that use electronic and computer effects," says Coppola. "So we decided to use our own naive effects, and that would give the film almost a mythical soul."

He is referring to a whole range of within-the-camera and onstage, or "floor," effects that date back to the earliest days of moviemaking. The birth of cinema coincided with the time frame of the Dracula story, and those early techniques suited Coppola's approach to the story. This *Dracula* comes from the age of magic and illusion and smoke and mirrors.

Coppola's chief collaborator in this experiment was his son Roman, the film's second unit director and visual effects director. "Roman is an expert on magic and photographic effects," says the director, "and we looked at some of the old silent films together."

Visual effects coordinator Alison Savitch also noted Roman Coppola's passion for old movie effects. "I think Roman has not only seen every movie made that had effects in it," she says, "he's read every article." Savitch oversaw all the "trick photography," while her counterpart on mechanical effects—the onstage sleight of hand—was Michael Lantieri.

Roman Coppola's research included tracking down old FX paraphernalia in camera shops and older technicians familiar with the techniques. He notes, "A lot of Victorian parlor amusements were optical tricks that developed into film. Stage magicians were among the first to buy projectors and cameras. We felt it would be unique to use techniques that no one has really seen in a long time."

These included running film in reverse (giving an off-kilter look to Lucy writhing on her bed), manipulating the frame of gravity (as when a drop of perfume falls upward in the Brides' chamber), multiple exposures (to show Harker's face and a train in the same frame). Various mirror effects were also explored, using 50-50 and angled mirrors, with images controlled by lighting—all of which hark back, Roman explains, to a patented stage illusion known as "Pepper's Ghost."

Some of the naive effects were suggested by classic films. Orson Welles, for example, was a master of mirrors. The dramatic shadow motifs found sources in German Expressionist cinema: Murnau's *Nosferatu*, of course, and especially the films of G. W. Pabst. Jean Cocteau's *Orpheus* inspired a shot combining rear projection with live action, where Dracula and Harker move along the castle hallway.

Using "old-fashioned" effects had many advantages. Results can be previewed instantly through the camera viewfinder without waiting for film to be processed or edited. Further, Roman points out, "the in-camera techniques, if they can do what you need, are better for quality; the film is pristine rather than being manipulated through several generations in the lab."

Not incidentally, they were great fun. Francis Coppola gave his effects crew great freedom: "Make it weird," he would say. Recalls Alison Savitch: "Francis didn't limit us in any way. His desire to try anything motivated us. All that freedom forces you to be creative, and that's the most fun in effects."

From Cocteau's Beauty and the Beast, *an inspiration for naive effects and set design.*

Miss Wilhelmina Murray
Hillingham Estate
Faversham
Kent
England

Closeup Dracula

DRACULA
Listen to them—the children of the night. What sweet music they make.

Back to Harker looking out the window. He turns back to Dracula. His frightened reaction:

His POV (normal-sized room) We see Dracula's long train snaking out the doorway, as the door closes by itself. The doorlocks clank in place; then his shadow moves across the room. (Music cue.)

Medium Harker (on rig—gravity shot) He sinks at the window in total fear. Soft rustling outside startles him. He turns and leans out to investigate. Over his shoulder we see: the sheer castle wall, river below. We move in tighter as a dark figure slowly emerges from a window, face down, its cloak spreading around it like great wings. It hesitates, then crawls sideways and scurries lizardlike through patches of moonlight down the wall.

Medium shot—Harker He ducks back. Then looks again.

[Castle wall—night—continuing action]

Harker's POV No figure. The wall impossible to climb.

Jump to Harker Writing in journal. He turns away, and we move in on the journal.

[Castle—guest quarters—night]

HARKER (V.O.)
"I did as Dracula instructed. I wrote three letters: to the firm, to my family, and to my beloved Mina. I said nothing of my fears, as he will read them, no doubt."

DRACULA
Good.

High angle shot
He begins to shave the rest of the petrified Harker's face. Camera booms down to low-angle two-shot, as the walls slowly close in.

DRACULA
Should you leave these rooms, you will not by any chance go to sleep in any other part of the castle. It is old, and has many bad memories. Be warned!

Close shot
The razor—we see the crucifix in the reflection.

HARKER
I'm sure I understand.

Close shot—Dracula
His eyes flash, fixing on the crucifix. He releases Harker and backs away. (The walls come back).

DRACULA
Do not put faith in such trinkets of deceit. We are in Transylvania, and Transylvania is not England. Our ways are not your ways, and to you there shall be many strange things.

On Harker
Harker turns, moving to window, anything to escape. His POV: down to the courtyard far below. Howling wolves echo offscreen in the distance.

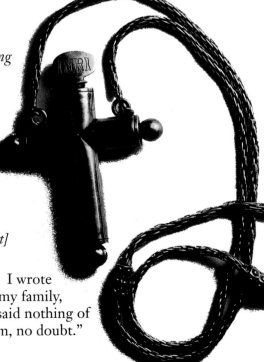

Prop of Dr. Van Helsing's crucifix. The ball at the top unscrews from the hollow body, which holds "holy water."

Cover from a 1916 edition of Dracula. *David Skal notes in* Hollywood Gothic *that the image of Dracula scaling the castle wall was not used in any stage or film adaptation until 1977.* Opposite: *Harker ventures deeper into the castle.*

HARKER (V.O.)
"I know now that I am a prisoner—and somehow being held so that this fiend can approach Mina. I understand little other than that I must return to her without delay. I fear for her—he must never meet her."

High angle
Below, Harker moves quickly away. We track along the ceiling, looking down at Harker past a statue in foreground. He hears women's rustle and laughter.

Low wide angle—tracking
behind Harker as he approaches a door with some Turkish script above it. Harker puts his elbow to the door. It gives a little.

Low medium angle—Harker in profile
He tries again, and the wooden door drags on the floor. It finally opens and he falls into the room.

[Ladies' quarters—night]

On Harker's back
He comes up, and we discover the room with him: the portion of the castle occupied by the ladies in bygone days. The room itself is a sumptuous tent and seraglio. Harker is frightened and wary. He moves and we track with him to an old and beautiful vanity. We lose him and track into the vanity: exquisite combs and brushes, powders. Perfume bottles and a mirror.

HARKER
Here some fair lady surely received the Count's pleasure.

Close shot—perfume bottle (gravity shot)
Harker opens it, and a drop of perfume hangs on the edge and finally drips upwards.

Wider—behind Harker
The drop of perfume flies up (reverse action). We hear female gasps, erotic sighs, whispers in Roumanian. Harker looks up, unsure if he saw anything.

Harker turns around
but sees nothing. We pan with him as he sits exhausted on pillows. The shadows from the moonlight against the leaves play on the silks hanging like great screens above him.

The light changes and we see Harker crouching at the door, trying to jimmy the lock. It clicks.

[Castle corridor—night]

Tracking shot 3/4
in front of Harker, exiting the room cautiously. Suddenly, the door startles him by swinging shut with a loud noise. He begins moving down the corridor. (Note: scary foreground pieces between camera and Harker—metal rods, reinforcements, etc.) He stops suddenly by the end, walking into closeup.

His POV
On a beam on the ceiling, we see rats scurrying upside down (gravity trick).

Insert:
Dracula crawling down the castle wall.

Insert:
Lizard in closeup.

Over his shoulder
He touches some of the beautiful fabric, then puts his face in it and smells it. The fabric starts moving on its own, like bedsheets inviting him in. They move, undulating like a woman. He pulls them back, but they are empty.

Closeup Harker
He turns.

His POV—panning shot
The indentation of tiny, feminine feet pressing themselves on the soft carpet. Then through the dust on the floor, zils playing.

Wide shot—Harker
sitting on pillows. Shadows move up the silks behind him.

Close shot—profile of Harker's chest
He grows very sleepy. We see a young

From Francis Coppola's journal:

"If all the peasants are telling you, 'Beware Castle Dracula! Don't go, don't go tonight, please, whatever you do—' and you go anyway because you've got business, and then you get to this creepy castle, and this guy who is a little weird and certainly looks strange is getting to you. But you're thinking, 'Well, but he sets you at ease.' How is Dracula going to set Harker at ease? Maybe he does it with a great wine and the treasures he shows him, and the implication of chicks later on. . . . He's seducing Harker. And that repressed Victorian sexuality becomes a force that works for Dracula . . . with both Harker and Mina. They're depraved on account of being deprived."

As I leaned from the window my eye was caught by something moving a storey below me, and somewhat to my left, where I imagined, from the order of the rooms, that the windows of the Count's own room would look out. . . . What I saw was the Count's head coming out from the window. I did not see the face, but I knew the man by the neck and the movement of his back and arms. In any case I could not mistake the hands which I had had so many opportunities of studying. I was at first interested and somewhat amused, for it is wonderful how small a matter will interest and amuse a man when he is a prisoner. But my very feelings changed to repulsion and terror when I saw the whole man slowly emerge from the window and begin to crawl down the castle wall over that dreadful abyss, face down with his cloak spreading about him like great wings. At first I could not believe my eyes. I thought it was some trick of the moonlight, some weird effect of shadow; but I kept looking, and it could be no delusion. I saw the fingers and toes grasp the corners of the stones, worn clear of the mortar by the stress of years, and by thus using every projection and inequality move downwards with considerable speed, just as a lizard moves along a wall.

What manner of man is this, or what manner of creature is it in the semblance of man?

woman's (Youngest Bride) hands come out of the fabric; the hands start touching him and caressing him. He joins in with his own hands so we see four hands caressing his chest. Then suddenly the woman's hand slits his shirt with a fingernail, and her hands rip open his shirt to his waist.

Close shot—Harker
He sits up. Looks forward with incredulity.

Harker's POV—Dracula's exquisite brides
Two are watching over him like adoring angels; the third moving backwards into the group.

THIRD BRIDE
(*Roumanian, to youngest*)
Go on. You are first, and we shall follow.

MIDDLE BRIDE
(*Roumanian*)
He is young and strong. There are kisses for us all.

Back to Harker
His reaction.

Harker's POV
The head of the Youngest Bride rising out of the fabric. The fabric falls, revealing her face. She works her way up his body, kissing his body, flicking her tongue up his stomach—camera pulls slowly back to over Harker on youngest bride—up his throat to his crucifix.

Her POV—the crucifix
around Harker's neck. Her face enters frame, smiling, then she reacts, seeing the crucifix. Suddenly she bites it in two like an animal. Camera turns as the crucifix slides off and disappears.

High angle—overhead shot
The Youngest Bride leans back, her hands on Harker's thigh. Harker's hands caress her body. Suddenly the fabric underneath him and around his head starts moving and it reveals the Middle Bride (reverse action trap door).

Closeup—Harker's chest in profile
Middle Bride's mouth and tongue come into frame. She licks and caresses Harker's nipple. Suddenly her white teeth bite his tit. His blood spurts into her red lips like a water fountain.

Closeup—Harker
reacting in ecstasy and pain.

Superimpose: extreme closeup
Tiny feet with golden zil cymbals welded on. Multi-image with zils.

Low angle
on Middle Bride, looking up at her like some Medusa with snakes for hair—the scars of impalement visible. Horrible sexual shadows behind her.

Low angle
The three of them entangled; grotesque and erotic shadows.

Close shot—Youngest Bride
Kisses and love bites on his wrist. Then she feeds from his wrist.

Superimpose: close shot
Her limpid purple eye.

Superimpose: wide shot
In the mirror above Harker we see only Harker's undulating reflection as he exalts.

Over Harker
The fabric between his legs bulges higher and higher, and the Middle Bride emerges as though born from him. His passion freed! The other Brides converge on Harker, their mouths finding each other in a torrid four-way kiss.

Wall with the stairs (short lens)
We see Dracula's shadow suddenly grow immense. He flies furiously through the window as it bursts open.

DRACULA
What is this!?

Back to four-way kiss
Dracula's shadow falls on the four-way kiss. A hand comes in and pulls off the Eldest Bride.

Brides' POV—low wide angle on Dracula
Tremendous, over them (special costume and rig). Dark, wind around him (reverse action), fire effect from the fireplace, so that he looks like the devil himself. He bends down and grabs the Youngest Bride and throws her—hurling her away like a rag doll.

DRACULA
(Roumanian)
How dare you touch him! When I have forbidden it—This man belongs to me!

The wall and ceiling (gravity shot)
She sticks to it—like a fly! She scurries across the ceiling, taunting Dracula, laughing, cruel—soulless.

The other Brides
laugh with her, then entwine themselves like a giant insect and scurry away together.

YOUNGEST BRIDE
(Roumanian)
You yourself never loved; you never love!

The scene with Harker and the Brides featured a specially constructed bed with a trap door that allowed them to emerge from beneath him. Overleaf: "I could hear the churning sound of her tongue as it licked her teeth and lips, and could feel the hot breath on my neck."

DRAPING DRACULA'S BRIDES

The Brides, left to right: Florina Kendrick, Monica Bellucci, and Michaela Bercu.

One of the few costumes that didn't meet with the director's immediate approval was Eiko's original idea for Dracula's vampire brides.

"Eiko's concept was to take the three naked girls and paint them green," Coppola recalls. "I guess she was thinking of the Green Fairy, the succubus (an image from the later absinthe scene), but it didn't work. It looked more like an art piece than a character."

Once Eiko realized that Coppola had a specific concept for the Brides, she tried to fulfill his ideas precisely. "He wanted a decaying, deteriorating feel to the fabric, like the shrouds of the mummies in the catacombs of Bombay. The passage of time would have turned the white fabric into a rich amber, and made it so fragile that it would crumble when you touch it.

"At the same time, he wanted extremely feminine robes, like the ones worn by the women in paintings by the French poster artist Mucha. I processed all this input and arrived at the final design for the Brides."

Dracula—camera tracks in
He recoils. His voice a soft tender whisper . . .

DRACULA
(Roumanian)
Yes—I too can love. And I shall love again.

Wide high angle—looking down on mosaic floor
The huge face of Elizabeth. The brides crawl seductively to him, folding themselves into him like a big furry animal.

YOUNGEST BRIDE
(Roumanian)
Are we to have nothing tonight?

Closer shot—low angle
Dracula turns away and then back, now holding a newborn infant in his palms. He presents it to the Brides, who swell with hunger and rush off to feast on it.

Closeup Harker
He chokes back his repulsion.

Medium closeup Dracula
He faces Harker—eyes blazing red. He makes an elegant, imperious gesture—

DRACULA
(Roumanian)
I promise you, when I am done with him, you shall "kiss" him at your will.

Medium Harker
He screams and falls back, fainting dead away.

Closeup Dracula
He laughs slowly and evilly.

Close to black through a square aperture; open the same way to:

[Hillingham garden—day]

Insert:
Harker's letter to Mina.

Track in
on Mina, visibly upset, reading the letter.

HARKER (V.O.)
"Dearest Mina, all is well here. The Count has insisted I remain for a month to tutor him in English custom. I can say no more, except I love you. Ever faithful, Jonathan."

She looks at the letter in the strange envelope and then to her side.

High angle
on Hillingham House. We boom down to see the family chapel and cemetery. We hear Lucy's mischievous laughter as she enters behind Mina, beautiful in a white lawn frock and full of excitement.

LUCY
I love him! There. That does me good to say it. I love him and I've said "yes."
(proclaiming)
Lord Arthur Holmwood. Lord and Lady Holmwood. You are to be my maid of honor. Oh, say "yes."

On Mina over Lucy
Mina doesn't react. Lucy notices.

LUCY
Mina, what is it? This is the most exciting day of my life, and you don't seem to care.

MINA
It's just that I am so terribly worried about Jonathan. His letter is so unnatural—so cold. It's not like him at all.

LUCY
Oh, Mina—don't worry.

Medium wide two-shot—steadicam
Thunder cracks unexpectedly. A cloudburst unloads, drenching them. Lucy revels in the downpour. Mina becomes more animated.

The rain and darkness move upon the maze. The two girls are frightened by the thunder and lightning. They look back to the sky. (Intercut begins.)

Insert—Dracula's eyes in the sky.
He smiles. Storm movement.

Mina's POV—wide shot
(Music in—the storm.)
An ominous, iridescent fog bank obscures the sunset. Brightened by flashes of lightning, it rolls toward them. Something powerful is coming.

Dissolve to:
[Castle chapel, crypt—day]

We start on black
It's a black box being filled with earth by two gypsies. It moves, revealing the chapel. Dim light streams down from the crumbling

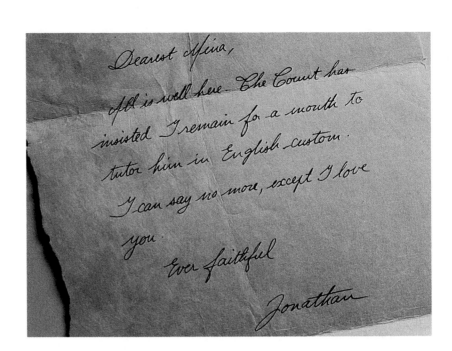

Dearest Mina,
All is well here. The Count has insisted I remain for a month to tutor him in English custom. I can say no more, except I love you.
Ever faithful
Jonathan

Mina Murray's Journal

26 July.—I am anxious, and it soothes me to express myself here; it is like whispering to oneself and listening at the same time. Also there is something about the shorthand symbols that makes it different from writing. I am unhappy about Lucy and about Jonathan. I had not heard from Jonathan in some time, and was very concerned . . . only a line dated from Castle Dracula that says he is starting for home. That is not like Jonathan; I do not understand it, and it makes me uneasy. Then, too, Lucy . . . has lately taken to her old habit of walking in her sleep. Her mother has spoken to me about it, and we have decided that I am to lock the door of our room every night. Mrs. Westenra has got an idea that sleep-walkers always go out on roofs of houses and along the edges of cliffs, and then get suddenly wakened and fall over with a despairing cry. . . .

6 August.—Another week gone, and no news from Jonathan. . . . Last night was very threatening, and the fishermen say that we are in for a storm. . . . The horizon is lost in a grey mist. All is vastness; the clouds are piled up like giant rocks, and there is a "brool" over the sea that sounds like some presage of doom.

vaulted ceiling. We track and see that the floor is broken.

HARKER (V.O.)
"Journal entry, 15th June. I hear below the sound of many tramping feet and the crash of weights being set down heavily."

We track across the floor and slowly tilt up to see Harker, watching gypsies from behind an iron grate covering a passageway.

His POV—the chapel below
The ruins of the same 14th-century altar where young Prince Dracula cradled Elizabeth.

HARKER (V.O. CONTINUED)
"The Count has a lowly group of gypsies enslaved to him. Day and night they toil, filling boxes with decrepit earth from the bowels of the castle. Earth? Why do they fill these boxes with earth?"

On Harker
He has made his way to the floor of the crypt, where stakes still protrude from the ground—skeletons, centuries old, with remnants of vestments and jewelry, grotesquely skewered on them. In the background we see the gypsies coming down the stairs, carrying out more boxes. We pull back and see Harker retreating and hiding behind one of the columns.

HARKER (V.O. CONTINUED)
"They are affixing the labels I brought with me to have the earth sent to his newly acquired Carfax Abbey in London, as part of some hideous scheme—and I am his accomplice!"

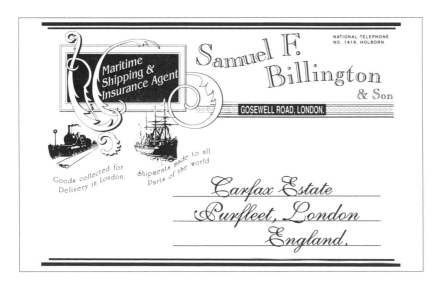

National Telephone No. 1419, Holborn.

Maritime Shipping & Insurance Agent

Samuel F. Billington & Son

GOSEWELL ROAD, LONDON.

Goods collected for Delivery in London.

Shipments made to all Parts of the world

Carfax Estate Purfleet, London England.

Closeup Harker
He takes shelter behind a stone coffin.

HARKER (V.O. CONTINUED)
"Soon the boxes will be sent aboard ship to London. The horrors grow more unspeakable as this journal proceeds."

Wider shot
Harker slowly peers over the top of Dracula's coffin, then climbs on top to examine it more closely.

Top of coffin moving
Panels pull apart to reveal Dracula laying in his "day coma" packed in the moldy earth; eyes wide open and stony. No sign of life.

HARKER (V.O.)
"This was the being I was helping to transfer to London, where—perhaps for centuries to come—he might amongst its teeming millions satiate his lust for blood, and create a new and widening circle of semi-demons to batten on the helpless."

The coffin
Dracula's inert body rises straight up, facing Harker.

On Harker
He stumbles back, sloshing through ankle-deep water, entangling himself in the skeletons, almost impaling himself. He hits a wall of catacombs.

Side angle—profile shot
Silvery laughter and bells echo. Dracula's laughter as the hands of the three Brides come out of their catacombs in the wall and grab Harker. We track around as he tries to get away, pulling them partially out. They arouse him, tantalizing him into the wall graves.

On coffin
Dracula's rigid form descends back into coffin; doors close. Fade to black.

Dracula's Harem: Casting and Choreographing the Brides

Finding the right women to play Dracula's insatiable Brides, and training them to move like supernatural creatures, was one of the film's major challenges. Francis Coppola felt that the Brides had never been portrayed cinematically as Stoker had drawn them—they were either scary or seductive, but not both—and in early casting discussions he played with some intriguing ideas.

"I may cast nine girls for this," he noted. "In other words: not just one woman for each character, but three actresses, three dancers, and three soft-core porn queens, or models. We would ask dancers to achieve things that an untrained person couldn't do . . . . Another possibility is that one of the Brides might be an older sexy woman—someone who is in her late fifties but still has that *je ne sais quoi*. . . .

"They should be ethnic types: Russian, Mongolian, Balkan, even Ethiopian. The Turkish sultan's wives came from all these places, and it's logical that Vlad could have met these types."

After a search consuming several months—600 actresses tried out in several cities around the country—the Brides were cast. There were just three after all, two models and all young but with very exotic looks. Italian actress and model Monica Bellucci was joined by Israeli model Michaela Bercu, making her film debut, and Romanian actress Florina Kendrick.

The Brides in action, pursuing their favored prey, Jonathan Harker.

In a stroke of serendipity, Florina was actually born in Transylvania and spoke fluent Romanian. She coached lead actors Oldman, Ryder, and Hopkins in the language, as well as her fellow Brides.

Coppola then enlisted the aid of Tony Award-winning choreographer Michael Smuin to stage strange and exotic movement for the Brides. "They were gorgeous beyond belief," Smuin says, "but they weren't dancers. But it wasn't necessarily 'dancing' that Francis wanted. It was more like ceremonial walking on air and walls and ceilings, and flying. At one point he said, 'Take these three girls and make them into a spider.' So with belts and loops and ropes we managed to put some interesting things together—certainly weird, yet beautiful and grotesquely lyrical."

The three actresses worked hard to develop the strength and agility to accomplish what Coppola and Smuin asked of them. "What came out was much better than I though possible," says the choreographer. And in keeping with the film's visual effects, "it was all done on camera; nothing was fake or done in the lab or with blue screen. It was all there."

The Brides' costumes and the set dressing for their chamber supported Coppola's idea that Dracula—a prince influenced by the East—kept a harem. "That's what the Koran is about," he declares, tongue firmly in cheek, "how to live with a lot of women in the house."

Above: *Mina and Lucy are rained on in the garden maze.* Opposite: *Keepers hose down the asylum inmates, as Dr. Seward prepares his injection.*

Closeup
Rigging and sails.

Insert:
Name of the ship painted on the bows: *Demeter*

Dissolve to:
[Hold of the *Demeter*—evening]

Camera swings by
in the hold of the schooner *Demeter*. Lantern swings wildly to and fro. Water streams down, spattering like drums on the stacks of Dracula's boxes as camera moves past them.

[Garden maze—evening]

Back to the girls
in the maze. Lucy chases Mina around the maze, both squealing like schoolgirls. Their horseplay becomes more intimate.

Close shot—Mina and Lucy
A kiss. They move away, without a word.

Steadicam in maze—various views
Lucy revels in the downpour, twirling, pulling her drenched white frock down over her body—transparent. Projections of storm clouds are cast onto Mina's diaphanous dress.

[London Zoo—storm continuing]

High wide angle
Camera swoops like a wave into the zoo, past the sign and by agitated animals.

Close shot
A great grey wolf whirls in its cage.

[Seward's asylum—storm continuing]

High angle shot
Camera swoops down on inmates as they howl and tear at each other and their barred windows. Keepers hose water on the inmates. We end close on one inmate, crouched in a corner of his cell: Renfield.

RENFIELD
Gather round, my pets; the Master of all life is at hand—

He senses the presence of a mighty force.

RENFIELD
Master, Master . . . I am here to do your

Cut to:
[Library]

Van Helsing opens a volume, narrates off-screen:

VAN HELSING
I will now read from the log of the *Demeter*, a sailing vessel: "27th June, 1897. We picked up 50 boxes of experimental earth bound for London, England. Set sail at noon into a storm that seemed to come out of nowhere, carrying us out to sea."

[Ocean—day]

A ship with torn rigging rides the stormy sea helplessly; the sky growing darker.

bidding, Master. I have worshiped you long and far off. Now that you are near—I am your slave—I await your commands. *Dumnezeu*. The blood is the life. *Dumnezeu*. The blood is the life!

He exults at the storm, summoning it like a conductor summons his orchestra. He rips the fastening of his straightjacket, and his ravings continue offscreen over Seward.

SEWARD (V.O.)
"The case of Renfield grows more interesting. . . ."

Dissolve to:
[Seward's office—storm continuing]

Medium closeup—Jack Seward
dictating into an Edison recorder. He is preparing an injection.

SEWARD
(dictating)
"Had I the secret of even one such brilliant mind—the key to the fancy of one lunatic—

The wolfen Dracula escapes from the Demeter; *original art by Sätty from* The Annotated Dracula.

(a rush of sorrow)
Lucy . . . since my rebuff, nothing seems of sufficient importance. Work is my cure. If only I had a strong cause as my poor mad friend, Renfield. . . .

Medium closeup—side angle
Seward ties off his arm. The injection is for himself. We move in on him; he swoons as

the drug courses through his veins, his face contorted. Thunder rolls. Lightning!

[Ocean—day]

The *Demeter* rides the storm-lashed sea.

[Hold of the Demeter*]*

Track in on box with royal crest. Intercut with painting of young Dracula. Voiceover of ship's log resumes:

VAN HELSING
"22 July. Second mate has gone missing. Passed Gibraltar. Storm continues; crew uneasy, believes someone or something is aboard the ship with us."

[Dracula's box—interior]

Dracula in day coma. We move in on him. He is a chrysalis in the shape of a man: shining, translucent, pulsing with life. An incredible metamorphosis is beginning. Fresh muscle, new bone, blood vessels constitute before us.

Francis Coppola on depicting the storm sequence:

"You could show the storm as a human storm. A storm in the asylum, shown in the behavior of the inmates. . . . Dracula's coming to England is throwing everything out of kilter. It's like the moon coming a little too close. All of the lower creatures and insane people are stimulated; it's almost sexual. Any intuitive beings—maybe Dracula affects them more.

" 'The master has come, the blood is the life. . . .' This is like a musical thing. The storm is building and building and reaches its high point with Dracula's arrival. It's organizing the film as though it were music."

Insert:
Portrait of young Dracula.

Insert:
Face of wolf-beast Dracula emerges from chrysalis, gnashes bloody jaws.

[Ocean—day]
Voiceover resumes:

VAN HELSING
The last entry is 3rd August. "Straits of Dover. At midnight I went to relieve first mate at the wheel, but he was not there. I shall tie my hands to the wheel. If I die, I pray this log may be found."

[Zoo—continuing action]
Wolf and other animals grow more agitated. Wolf escapes.

Insert:
Moon, sailing fast through clouds.

Dissolve to:
[Hillingham—storm continuing]

Swooping wide shot
The front of Hillingham in the storm.

Dracula's wolfen snarl rises from the estate cemetery.

[Lucy's bedroom—storm continuing]

MINA (V.O.)
"Diary again. Lucy, although she is so well, has lately taken to her old habit of walking in her sleep. Fortunately, the weather is so hot that she cannot get cold; but still the anxiety is beginning to tell on me, and I am getting nervous and wakeful myself."

Angle on window
It blows open. Curtains fly in. Mina enters from right, in her bedclothes. We pan her to the bed.

MINA
Lucy—are you all right—

She can't see in the dark. She feels the bed—empty. She notices Lucy's crucifix is left on the bed. Covers tossed on the floor. She runs to the open window.

Insert—Lucy's crucifix on the bed

Closeup Mina

Mina discovers that Lucy is missing.

Worried, she peers out the window.

Mina's POV—wide shot
Descending the long steps to the cemetery, Lucy, her gown rippling and blowing about her—

Double-exposure: Dracula's face.

[Cemetery—storm continuing]

Tracking Lucy 3/4 behind her
Sleepwalking through the maze, then up more steps.

Closeup tracking in front of Lucy
Serene smile. Oblivious to the winds ripping at her.

High angle on Mina
pursuing Lucy through maze.

"Whenever you do a movie," Francis Coppola explains, "the director asks himself, how can I use the period or place of the story to influence the style? Since *Dracula* took place around the turn of the century, I started looking at the art of that period, and settled on the Symbolist period in painting as one that would give us great visual opportunity to get into the mood and themes of the story. So I went through many many pictures and books, and prepared a notebook to show my art directors and Eiko."

Symbolism was a late 19th-century movement in the literary and visual arts that drew heavily on myth, fantasy, and historical references. It expressed a *fin de siècle* mood of uneasiness and melancholy; an aesthetic reaction to the growing power of science and industry; an erotic

Above: Tragedy *by Gustav Klimt, c. 1897.* Below, left: *Klimt's* Judith II, *c. 1909.*

rebellion against bourgeois propriety. Many Symbolist artists externalized images from the realm of the unconscious. Some sought escape in dreams through drug-taking or absinthe.

The expressive language of Symbolism is "a kind of evocative, poetic use of imagery," as Coppola puts it, "almost a dream state." This quote

from the French poet Verlaine conveys the tone that Symbolism shares with Coppola's film: "I love the word 'decadence,' all gleaming with crimson. . . . It is made up of a mixture of carnal spirit and melancholy flesh, and all the violent splendors of the Byzantine Empire."

Among the painters whose work chiefly inspired *Dracula's* design team are Gustav Klimt, Caspar David Friedrich, Gustave Moreau, and Fernand Khnopff. Eiko Ishioka recalls that "Francis's desk was piled high with research material." Individual images clearly inspired some details of the set decoration for Dracula's castle and the Hillingham crypt, the Brides' flowing hair and costumes, and Lucy's ethereal-erotic look as the vampire's willing victim.

Indeed, the world that Dracula inhabits is familiar territory to the Symbolist imagination—whose artists, in the words of Moreau, "hurl themselves into the abysses of bygone ages, into the tumultuous spaces of dreams and nightmares."

Obsession, *by the Polish Symbolist Wojciech Weiss, c. 1899-1900.*

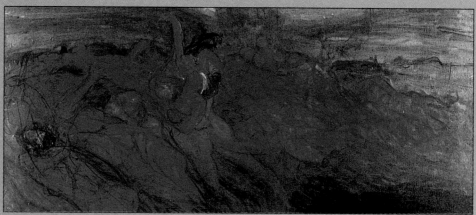

Loose tracking shot
Mina emerges from the fog wrapped in a shawl, fighting wind and spray. She comes closer and walks into her closeup. She stops dead as the howling reaches her.

MINA
Lucy! Lucyyyy!

A stab of lightning illuminates the cemetery.

Mina's POV—wide shot (head-on)
Lucy's figure is splayed wantonly on a stone bench, her arms pinned back, her hips undulating wildly. A dark figure, erect like a wet man or beast bends over her—mounts her between her legs.

Closeup
Fangs in Lucy's bloodied neck.

Medium two-shot—Dracula and Lucy
Then he slowly rears up and turns, staring with flashing red eyes.

Medium closeup
Mina in the mist, watching, frozen.

Dracula's POV—pixilation
View moves into Mina.

DRACULA (V.O.)
No . . . do not see me—

Closeup Dracula
Very emotional about seeing her; almost stunned.

His POV of Mina
Explosion of lightning, blinding the view. Frame goes white.

"There was undoubtedly something, long and black, bending over the half-reclining white figure. . . . What it was, whether man or beast, I could not tell. . . I called in fright, 'Lucy! Lucy!' and something raised a head, and from where I was I could see a white face and red, gleaming eyes."

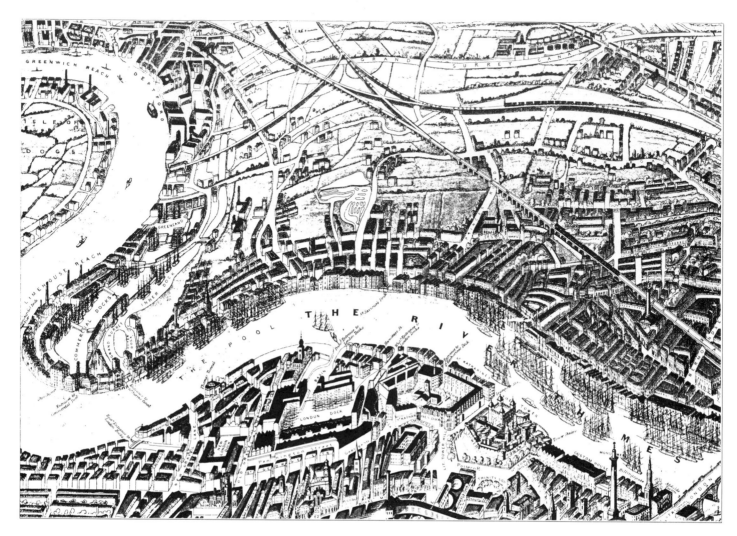

Dracula's map of London.

[Cemetery—storm continuing]

Mina's POV—medium shot

Lucy alone, breathing in heavy, orgasmic gasps; gown spread, revealing her breasts—her thighs. Mina runs into the POV, wraps her shawl about Lucy, pinning it at her neck. Track around and in as she shakes Lucy hard, waking her into a half-dreamy state.

Lucy

His eyes . . . eyes . . .

Mina

It's all right. You were dreaming—walking in your sleep again.

Lucy

Please don't tell anyone—please.

Mina

Shush up. Let's get you home.

Mina stands her up; we track back as she

takes Lucy home. The view alters, revealing Dracula watching them, still paralyzed by emotion.

Insert—pendulum shot of Carfax Abbey

[Carfax—day]

Close shot

A box on a crane; we see the Billington shipping logo. The box swings away from camera; camera moves back and up so that we see, from high angle, lorrymen unloading boxes from two delivery wagons marked "Carter, Patterson & Son," and taking them into the Carfax Chapel.

Van Helsing reads in voiceover:

Van Helsing (v.o.)

For the record, I enter a letter from the Count to Samuel F. Billington and Son.

Dracula (v.o.)

"Dear Sirs, you will please deposit the

boxes, 50 in number, to Carfax Estate, near Purfleet, in the partially ruined abbey. Faithfully yours, Count Dracula."

Dissolve to:
[Carfax—exterior]

From long view on Carfax, camera pulls back to asylum, outside:

[Renfield's cell—storm continuing]
On Renfield
Through his high, barred window.

RENFIELD
Master! I am here! Master . . . !

[Carfax chapel interior—day]
Wide low angle
The boxes lined up in the ruined chapel. We track along them and track in on the royal seal of Dracula's box.

Insert:
Dracula in chrysalis form, changing again.

Insert:
Map of London that we saw at Castle Dracula, with the location of Carfax marked in red.

VAN HELSING (V.O.)
The vampire, like any other night creature, can move about by day—though it is not his natural time and his powers are weak.

"The Master has come!"

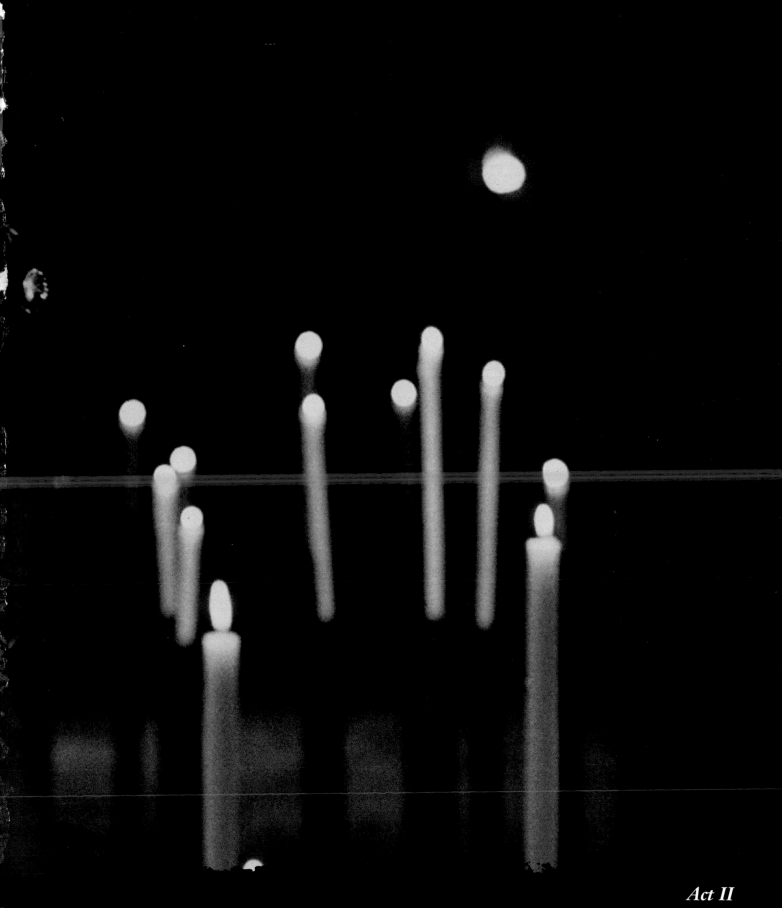

Act II

The Blood Is the Life

[*London street—afternoon*]

Dracula's POV—tracking,
(Pathé camera produces slightly jerky, speeded-up movement of early silents. Music cue.) Scanning the rush of humanity out for a Sunday stroll. Women in great hats parade by with and without gentlemen. Each woman steals a glance at us, looking into the lens.

Closeup—Young Dracula
In broad daylight! Positively the most dashing, handsome man on the street. His eyes hidden behind the newest fashion—tinted glasses. He smiles with perfect white teeth, tipping his hat to each woman who catches his eye.

NEWS HAWKER (O.S.)
Suddenest and greatest storm on record strikes England . . . Escaped wolf from zoo still at large!

Medium wide shot—Dracula
As he walks, he avoids direct sunlight.

Closer shot on Dracula
His eyes are following someone. (Music cue.)

Dracula's POV—Mina in the crowd
(*Long lens, high speed 24-40, background goes darker; compensate by putting light on Mina.*) Tense, preoccupied as she hurries through the crowd. Her eyes meet his. She looks immediately away. Something compels her to look again.

Medium close Dracula
as he stops and stares across the street at her.

DRACULA
(*whispers*)
See me now!

Mina abruptly enters an apothecary.

[*Apothecary—day*]

Dracula watches at the window. We see people's reflections, but not Dracula's. The News Hawker comes up to Dracula, sells him a paper.

Insert—newspaper

The *Pall Mall Gazette:* "Escaped Wolf" and "Record Storm."

Closeup Dracula
He looks up.

Dracula's POV
The window, Mina inside. In the reflection of the window we see the newspaper floating in midair.

On door
Mina, about to put the bottle into her bag, exits into two-shot and bumps right into . . . Dracula. The bottle drops—camera pans with the bottle and Dracula's hand catches it. We come up with the medicine back into two-shot.

Over shoulder Mina on Dracula

DRACULA
My humblest apologies. Forgive my ignorance. I am recently arrived from abroad and do not know your city. Is a beautiful lady permitted to give a "lost soul" directions?

Over shoulder Dracula on Mina
Intrigued by his manner and voice but properly put off.

MINA
For "lost souls" I would suggest Westminster Church. You may purchase a street atlas for sixpence. Good day.

Two-shot
She holds out her hand. He almost grasps it with his trembling hand, then realizes he has her medicine. He hands it to her; she adds it to her shopping bag.

DRACULA
Have you not the right as a modern woman to engage in an intelligent conversation of your own free will with whomever you choose?

MINA
(challenged)
Perhaps—but I choose not to.

We track with Mina. She pushes by him

The London street scenes were the shot on the Universal Studios back lot—the only outdoor location used in Dracula. "On those two days," marvels producer Chuck Mulvehill, "it rained. It was cloudy and overcast. It was perfect."

and walks away. We stay on Dracula as he bows politely, letting her go.

DRACULA
I have offended you. I am only looking for the cinematograph. I understand it is a wonder of the civilized world.

MINA
If you seek culture, visit a museum. London is filled with them. If you will excuse me?

Dracula's POV—Mina walking away

Empty shot
Mina enters frame. Camera pulls back in front of her to reveal Dracula in the foreground. Mina is shocked, indignant.

DRACULA
A woman so lovely and . . . intelligent should not be walking the streets of London without her gentleman.

MINA
Do I know you, sir? Are you acquainted with my husband? Shall I call the police?

DRACULA
I shall bother you no more.

He bows, defeated, and turns to leave.

Close on Mina
Mina is confused, fighting against every rule of decorum—

MINA
Sir, it is I who have been rude. The cinematograph is . . .

On Dracula
He turns back, grinning like a lovesick schoolboy.

DRACULA
Please. Permit me to introduce myself. I am Prince Vlad of Szeklys.

MINA
(with humor)
A prince, no less.

DRACULA
I . . . am your servant.

We track in front of Dracula to two-shot with Mina.

Associate Producer Susie Landau:

"Francis's ever-present drive to be authentic was very prevalent in this film. We had coaches for period movement and etiquette—both for lead actors and extras, for example in the party scene at Hillingham. An acting coach, Greta Seacat, worked with Winona and Sadie to help them connect the point of view of young Victorian women to their own experience. Dancing instruction for the waltzing scene, Romanian lessons for Gary and the Brides, and so on. We wanted to build in things that would make you feel that you're experiencing the history as it's happening, that you're part of a reality where past, present, and future meet all at once."

WHAT MAKES A VAMPIRE?

Over the centuries in which vampires have appeared in folklore, fiction, and films, there has been much confusion about just what a vampire is, and what he (or she) can and cannot do.

Physically, vampires through the ages tend to be very pale, with dark hair and red, burning eyes; tall, gaunt, and cadaverous of feature; sometimes cold to the touch—or, if female, hauntingly beautiful with very red, sensuous lips and lustrous

Max Schreck as Dracula in F.W. Murnau's 1922 film Nosferatu.

eyes. Typically they cast no shadow (though filmmakers have restored it to them!) and do not reflect in mirrors.

In early folklore, they kill their victims by biting their chests or suffocating them; later writers chose the neck as the point of entry. Most prefer young women, children, or beautiful young men. They often exert some hypnotic power that renders their victims willing.

Methods of dispatching vampires include the familiar staking, burning, and decapitation, as well as blood starvation, excising the heart, killing with a consecrated sword, and even removing the teeth! Short-term remedies are crucifixes, garlic, dogroses, holy water, the "holy circle," and the Host.

Vampires possess extraordinary strength and shape-shifting powers, though Dracula's appearance in the form of mist is unusual. Their powers are limited in vari-

ous ways; for instance, they generally must be invited to cross the threshold of a victim's house.

Can a vampire endure daylight? Most sources, based on ancient beliefs about night being the realm of evil, say no. Stoker is the exception: Dracula goes abroad during the day, though his powers are much diminished. ("He can only change himself at exact noon or at sunrise or sunset.") By contrast, Murnau's film *Nosferatu* withers to dust when struck by the first rays of dawn, and Anne Rice's modern fictional vampires must go to earth wherever they are.

Another point of divergence is how new vampires are made. Traditional lore has it that every person killed by a *nosferatu* also becomes a vampire after death. However, Stoker's fiction implies (and Rice's states explicitly) that there must be a *blood exchange* between vampire and victim—such as Mina drinking from Drac-

Medium closeup—Mina

MINA
Wilhelmina Murray—

Two-shot

DRACULA
It is I who am honored, Madam Mina.

She allows a tentative smile, charmed and disarmed. We see them turn and go back in the direction they came from, and the camera booms up to see Prince Dracula, barely containing his joy, escort Mina into the swirl of life on the streets of London. Streetlamps are being lit. Big Ben chimes. We see the giant shadow of the escaped wolf.

Dracula's walking stick (prop), ornamented with his trademark crest.

"A Man's Brain and a Woman's Heart"

Mina Harker, the heroic victim of Stoker's novel and Dracula's long-lost love in the Coppola film, is played by Winona Ryder—who also played a key role in bringing James Hart's screenplay to production.

Ryder had been reading scripts, seeking a role that would expand her reach beyond the teenage characters she has portrayed so effectively. She found it in the strong figure of Mina, who, while irresistibly drawn to Dracula, nonetheless joins the Vampire Killers in hunting him down. Her courage and resourcefulness inspire Dr. Van Helsing to say that she has "a man's brain and a woman's heart"—a compliment in Stoker's day. Jim Hart says, "The key to writing *Dracula* was to make it Mina's story."

"I had read *Dracula* in junior high school," Ryder recalls, "and the way it was told, through journals, was interesting to me because I've kept a journal pretty consistently since I was very young."

Meeting with Coppola on another project, Ryder left him the *Dracula* script and was both surprised and delighted when he wanted to direct it. She says, "I think Francis and I liked the same things about the script, which was very romantic and sensual and epic. . . . It's not really a vampire movie. To me it's more about the man Dracula, the warrior, the prince. He is unlike any other man—he's mysterious and very sexual—attractive in a dangerous way."

Named for her birthplace of Winona, Minnesota, Ryder moved with her family to northern California when very young and performed in her early teens with San Francisco's prestigious American Conservatory Theater. Since her film debut in *Lucas*, she has appeared in nine features including *Heathers*, *Great Balls of Fire*, *Mermaids*, and Jim Jarmusch's *Night on Earth*, as well as the Tim Burton movies *Beetlejuice* and *Edward Scissorhands*.

Ryder had to master an English accent and proper Victorian manners to play Mina—her research included watching period movies and "anything with Maggie Smith," as well as reading books on turn-of-the century etiquette. Yet she found a contemporary streak in the character. "She's very independent for her time," Ryder notes. "She has strength and intelligence, but her connection with Dracula is uncontrollable."

Cut to:
[Hillingham foyer—evening]

Bells chime the hour. Jack Seward enters, checking his watch. His hat, etc., taken by the butler Hobbs.

SEWARD
Mr. Holmwood asked me to stop by to see Miss Lucy.

Hobbs nods knowingly.

[Conservatory—evening]
Medium shot—Lucy
standing in front of a mirror by the window, as a woman fits her wedding dress.

HOBBS (O.S.)
Dr. Seward, Miss Lucy—

She turns, bubbling delight. . . . We track towards her.

LUCY
Jack—brilliant Jack. Do you like it?

She spins for approval; her skin a chalky white, weight loss frightening. Gaunt, cheeks sunken in, receding gums, but very sexy. The early stages of vampire transformation.

Medium closeup—Seward
Shocked at her appearance.

Medium shot—Lucy
Seward enters frame.

LUCY
Did Arthur put you up to this? Or did you want to be alone just once before I'm married?

Ever the tease, she toys with a choker around her neck. Seward forces a laugh, hiding his reaction. He takes her hand instead of her kiss and leads her to the chaise, ending in wider two-shot. He takes out his notebook.

SEWARD
Now, Lucy—you're embarrassing me—I'm here as your doctor. Your fiancé is very worried about you, and I assure you, a doctor's confidence is sacred. I must have your complete trust.

Closer two-shot
Lucy reclines on the chaise, hiding her eyes in her hands. (Music cue.)

Closeup Lucy

LUCY

Help me, Jack. Please, I don't know what's happening to me. I'm changing—I can feel it. I can hear everything—servants whispering at the other end of the house—mice in the attic, stomping like elephants . . . I'm having horrible nightmares, Jack . . . the eyes . . . I can see things in the dark plain as day—and I'm starving, but I cannot bear the sight of food. Help me—Jack—

She gasps, unable to breathe, clutching Seward.

Medium close Seward
preparing the injection.

SEWARD

I'm here, Lucy, nothing will harm you—

Camera moves back to include Lucy as he jabs the shot in her arm, stroking her cheek, trying to comfort the one he loves but has lost. Lucy moans—the drug taking effect.

LUCY
(moaning)
Oh, Jack   kiss me!

Drawn against his will, he does so.

[Hillingham—evening]

Low wide angle
Holmwood and Quincey arrive with their hunting party, on horseback. Spirits high, joking with one another. We pan with them to see Seward at the door.

On Holmwood
from his horse.

HOLMWOOD
Hello, Jack, and how's our lovely patient today?

On Seward
Seward is clearly at a loss for words.

SEWARD
Well, frankly, Arthur, I'm confounded.

Medium shot
Holmwood and Quincey dismount. We pan them to Seward.

Dr. Seward puzzles over Lucy's symptoms.

QUINCEY
(slaps him hard on the back)
Awww—brooding over Lucy again, Jack?

[Main hall—day]

Medium three-shot—tracking in front of them
Seward leads them into the main hall.

SEWARD
She has difficulty breathing—but no infection is present. She complains of nightmares that terrify her, but cannot remember them.

HOLMWOOD
Well, what do you make of it?

SEWARD
I can only conclude it must be something mental.

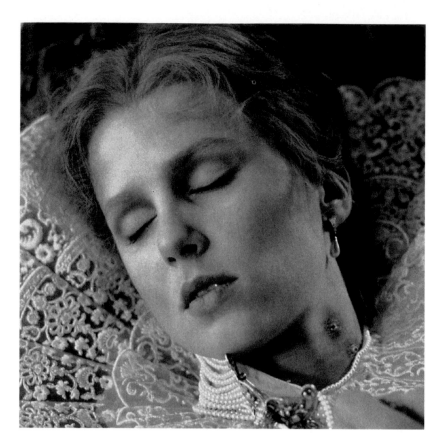

HOLMWOOD
Hear that, Quincey? Last week Jack wanted to marry her—this week he wants to have her committed. Let's go have a look, shall we?

Quincey and Holmwood laugh. They enter the conservatory.

[Conservatory—evening]
Men's POV—Lucy
sleeping fitfully.

View on men
Holmwood and Quincey react with shock to her grave condition. We track in on them, losing Seward.

Single on Seward

SEWARD
I am at a loss, I admit. I have taken the liberty of cabling Abraham Van Helsing, the metaphysician-philosopher. . . .

QUINCEY
He sounds like a goddamn witch doctor to me.

SORCERY ON SCREEN

Just before the turn of the century, a new fashion hit London: moving pictures. People would gather outside the cinematograph in long lines to witness this miraculous fusion of science and stage sorcery.

The *cinématographe*, a combination camera-projector, was developed in 1894 by Louis Lumière, one of the great French pioneers of cinema. It incorporated earlier inventions by Eadward Muybridge and especially Thomas Edison, whose Kinetoscope was capable of showing film in synchronization with a phonograph record. Edison's did not include a projector, however, so filmstrips could only be viewed by one per-

The battle between Romanians and Turks projected in puppet show.

son at a time, "peep show" style, through a hole in a box. Lumière's cinematograph, later exploited by stage magician Georges Méliès, projected images on a backdrop so that a whole audience could watch and wonder.

Méliès was also a puppeteer,

and many early films featured stories enacted by shadow puppets. This technique was revived and adapted by Coppola to stage the 15th-century battle sequence that opens *Dracula*. Projected silhouettes and more realistic puppets were used in the background and middle ground, in combination with foreground live action, to give a sense of depth and graphic impact to the scene.

Past, present, and future are joined in a sly cinematic joke, when this same sequence (set in 1462 and filmed in 1991) is screened at the cinematograph visited by Dracula and Mina in 1897 London.

SEWARD
Van Helsing knows more about obscure diseases than any man in the world. He was my teacher and mentor.

HOLMWOOD
Do it, man, bring him here. Spare no expense.

Closeup Lucy
on the chaise, sleeping, moaning. We track in a little as her hand rests on the choker, pulling it down, revealing two red marks.

Extreme closeup—the wounds
Two surgical wounds. We track in on the wounds.

Cut to:
[Early movie theater—evening]

Closeup—Queen Victoria
We pull back to see the projection of Queen Victoria in a carriage, celebrating her diamond jubilee.

Wide shot
We are in the cinematograph. Guests stand together in the small dark room, marveling at the screen, an early short subject. We move in on Mina, standing tentatively close to Dracula. He refers to the illusion on the screen.

DRACULA
Astounding. There are no limits to science.

On Mina over Dracula

MINA
How can you call this . . .
(referring to screen)
"science?" Do you think Madame Curie would invite such comparisons? Really!

On Dracula over Mina
Dracula laughs like a schoolboy, taking her all in. Mina suddenly realizes she is alone with this attractive man.

MINA
I shouldn't have come here. I must go.

Londoners at the cinematograph.

Mina encounters the wolf. In Stoker, the zookeeper tell us, "That 'ere wolf what we call Bersicker [Cockney for Berserker] was a-tearin' like a mad thing at the bars as if he wanted to get out. . . . Close at hand was only one man, a tall, thin chap with a 'ard, cold look and red eyes."

She starts to leave, but he is more aggressive. His hand is suddenly holding her.

DRACULA
Do not fear me.

Tracking shot
He is more forceful, pulling her deeper into the shadows of the cinematograph.

Two-shot silhouette
Mina is breathing heavily—frightened and excited, her emotions bursting out. Pulled to him in ways she doesn't understand.

MINA
No—please, stop this—stop this—

From Francis Coppola's journal:

"Everyone knows the phenomenon of trying to hold your breath underwater—how at first it's all right and you can handle it, and then as it gets closer to the time when you must breathe, how urgent the need becomes, the lust and the hunger to breathe. And then the panic that sets in when you begin to think that you won't be able to breathe—and finally, when you take in the air and the anxiety subsides . . . that's what it's like to be a vampire and need blood."

DRACULA
(whispers in Roumanian)
You are the love of my life.

MINA
(trembling in fear)
My God—who are you? I know you. . . .

DRACULA
Yes, you are she—the one I lost. I have crossed oceans of time to find you. . . .

Close two-shot
Dracula turns away from her toward camera, his great fangs fully extended like a serpent's. He bends close to her, his fangs about to sink into her pulsing neck. He is astonished at the emotion he feels; his fangs recede. His eyes burning red like lasers in the dark.

Single on wolf silhouette
moving down one of the side corridors, past the shadow puppet battle. A woman in the audience screams.

Wide shot—the wolf
behind them, moving down the corridor toward Mina. She breaks away from Dracula. We pan with her as she runs toward the screen. The wolf crosses in front of camera and stops, blocking her from the exit.

Hillingham at dusk. This is actually a model the size of a very large dollhouse.

Low angle wolf
curls its lips in a snarl. Dracula enters from left behind the wolf with a sweeping gesture, speaking his mother tongue.

DRACULA
Strigoi! Moroi!
The wolf cowers—understanding, whimpering.

From Francis Coppola's journal:

"When Dracula drops Mina off in the coach, maybe it's early evening, between 6 and 8—kind of a magical transition time where the lights are coming on. If you look at movies like *Limelight* and other films depicting Victorian times, there is a period of promenade in the early evening, when young women are heading home. It's not the same as being out with a strange guy late at night."

Medium closeup—Mina
The early film continues to play in the background, images flickering over beast and woman. Mina is too terrified to cry out—

On Dracula and wolf
Dracula beckons. Gentle. The great wolf comes, head down, obedient. He cradles the wolf's head in his white gloves, rubbing his ears, stroking his great back.

DRACULA
Come here, Mina. . . . Have no fear. . . .

Medium closeup—Mina
Mina resists, shaking her head violently no. Dracula enters frame left. He draws her hand in his. We track with them to the wolf. She struggles as he pulls her hand to the wolf—then her hand touches the soft fur.

Close shot
Hands on fur. She strokes its great neck.

DRACULA
He likes you.

Closeup Mina
She looks at Dracula, intoxicated, almost fainting. An unspoken understanding passes between them. The very image of Eliza-beth, Mina finds herself enchanted and full of trust as she pets the wolf.

Dracula
There is much to be learned from beasts.

Closeup Dracula
He removes his glasses; his eyes again crys-tal blue—

[Sky—night]

Close shot—the full moon

[Hillingham—moonlight]

Wide shot
(Music cue.) An elegant coach stops in front of the house. Dracula helps Mina down; moonlight glowing about her. We track with them into a two-shot favoring Mina. Mina lingers, reluctant for it to end. He savors the moon. Silence. Both fixed on each other, unable to move. He bends, kiss-ing her hand. Mina reaches to stroke his hair—like the wolf—then catches herself pulling back.

Track 3/4 behind Mina
As she walks to the entrance. A rush of sex-ual adrenalin. Her face flushed, unable to contain her excitement. She stops and turns back—

Mina's POV
Dracula is gone.

Fade out. Fade in:

Insert—Seward's telegram to Van Helsing about Lucy
spooling out of the telegraph:
"Come at once. Do not lose an hour. A dear friend near death. Disease of the blood unknown to all medical theory. I am in des-perate need. Jack Seward."

[Amsterdam—laboratory—day]

Microscopic view of blood
Pulsing. Cells churning. Corpuscles battle, attacking a foreign cell.

Low angle closeup
Abraham Van Helsing lecturing a handful of students. ("The poise of his head indi-cates thought and power . . . sculpted in mys-tery and kindness . . . dark blue eyes quick and tender or stern with the man's moods.")

Van Helsing
The tropical Pampas vampire bat must con-sume ten times its weight in fresh blood each day, or its own blood cells will die.

We pan to his thumb; he slits it with a lancet.

Closeup bat
Van Helsing's bleeding hand goes into a cage holding two small bats. The creatures fix themselves to his hand and suck his blood.

Van Helsing in his lec-ture hall.

87

Dr. Seward's Diary

When we were alone [Quincey] said to me: "Jack Seward, I don't want to shove myself in anywhere where I've no right to be; but this is no ordinary case. You know I loved that girl and wanted to marry her; but although that's all past and gone, I can't help feeling anxious all the same. What is it that's wrong with her? . . . I have not seen anything pulled down so quickly since I was on the Pampas and had a mare that I was fond of go to grass all in a night. One of those big bats that they call vampires had got at her in the night, and what with his gorge and the vein left open, there wasn't enough blood in her to let her stand up, and I had to put a bullet through her as she lay."

View on students
they react with audible shock as Van Helsing agitates the bats.

Low wide angle Van Helsing
He seems to enjoy the sucking, reveling in his effect on both bats and students. Jerking his hand away, he teases the bats with his bloody fingers, as we tilt up to his face.

VAN HELSING
Cute little vermin, *ja?*

Pull back to wider shot.

VAN HELSING
The blood—and the diseases of the blood . . . such as syphilis. The very name "venereal" diseases—the diseases of Venus—imputes to them divine origin. They are involved in that sex problem about which the ideals and ethics of Christian civilization are concerned. In fact, civilization and syphilization have advanced together. . . .

Students laugh nervously. An assistant enters, holding a telegram; comes over to Van Helsing.

VAN HELSING
Ja. . . . What is this?

ASSISTANT
It's from the telegraph, Professor.

VAN HELSING
Telegraph . . .
(reads it)
Thank you. That will be all, gentlemen. Good morning.

Students rap their knuckles on desktops in applause.

VAN HELSING
For the record, I do attest that at this point, I, Abraham Van Helsing, became personally involved in these strange events.

Insert—Castle Dracula—exterior

Dissolve to:
[*Castle Dracula—ladies' quarters—rainy day*]

A drop of blood rolls slowly across a stone surface.

Closeup—Youngest Bride
Her open mouth and bloody fangs.

High angle
Harker, splayed in crucified position at the window. He is almost nude; eyes sunken, hair starting to turn gray. A husk ravaged by fear and hunger—Brides entangled about him. Camera swoops slowly down as the youngest strokes him, licking blood off her fingers. His arrogance gone—his nightmare not over.

HARKER (V.O.)
"Dawn. These may be the last words I write in this journal. Dracula has left me with these women, these devils of the pit. They drain my blood to keep me weak, barely alive so I cannot escape. Today I wll try one last time — there is a way that is dangerous, but I may be able to escape to the river. . . . Oh, Mina, I wish I could see you one more time!

Pan down to mosaic of Elizabeth's face as voiceover concludes.

[*London/Hillingham—night*]

Dracula's POV—pixilation shot
Starts on London streets; we see some rats and cockroaches scurrying by.

[Hillingham—night]

Van Helsing's coach comes up the road. We see Hillingham in the background.

Wide low angle
Dense fog has set in. A coach stops in front of the house. Van Helsing steps out, carrying a valise. We see his shadow on the wall. The coach leaves, revealing Van Helsing standing there. He remains motionless, sensing, listening. Urgency sweeps over him. He ascends the steps hurriedly.

Pixilation POV
continues to the front of Hillingham (miniature), moves through the garden past a dead bird under a bush, and reveals the rear of Hillingham. POV leaps and glides to Lucy's balcony window.

DRACULA (V.O.)
(barely audible whisper)
Lucy . . . Lucy . . . Lucy . . . come!

[Lucy's bedroom—night—continuing action]

Close on Lucy's hand clutching the satin sheet, slowly drawing it up off her body.

Reverse on Dracula

Watching her through the window (miniature window—he fills the frame). He moves his hands over his body, gestures with a pulling motion, as if drawing her to him.

Francis Coppola on Dracula's unique POV:

"The predator's POV should always be scary, like it was in *Jaws*. I'd like to find something unique to represent that. Let's not just have an aerial view of some countryside; everyone has seen that shot of a vampire's point of view. I want to make us have less to do so that what we can do is very interesting."

Roman Coppola:

"We call it pixilation, Dracula's fast-moving POV. It's something like animation, and is produced by a device inside the camera that takes individual images. The trick is to click off frames erratically—single frames and then a burst of several per second—giving the effect of an animal-like sensory perception, something primordial."

Seward welcomes his mentor, Van Helsing.

Medium close overhead shot
on Lucy, turned away from camera. She senses the presence and turns over. Her eyes brighten. We pull back as she smiles wantonly and reveals her body.

Dracula's POV—Lucy
We pan up her body as she arouses herself with her own caress. Her hands glide up her body, finding her breasts. Pan ends on her neck as she removes her choker—stroking her neck slowly with her hands—then faster—ejaculatory . . . sexual powers awakened. This is what she has hungered for.

Over Lucy
on the elongated shadow of Dracula's claw-

like hands reaching toward her. As he approaches, a bouquet of flowers wilts instantly in a vase.

[Hillingham—entrance hall—continuing action]

Steadicam wide shot
We see Van Helsing enter in far background from right and Seward enter from left. Camera moves fast with Seward leading us into a two-shot .

SEWARD
Professor Van Helsing. How good of you to come.

Van Helsing, set in his eccentric ways, doesn't shake hands, but rather places his gloves and hat in Seward's care and immediately surveys the house with his sixth sense.

Already fearful of the power he is up against—

VAN HELSING
I always come to my friends in need when they call me. So, Jack—tell me everything about your case.

SEWARD
She has all the usual physical anemic signs—her blood analyzes normal—and yet—it is not. She manifests continued blood loss; I cannot trace the cause. . . .

VAN HELSING
(sharply)
Blood loss how?

[Hillingham—main room—night]

Tight two-shot from high angle
looking down at Van Helsing and Seward, deep in conversation. Shadows of the blossoms are cast by the moon onto the floor. Suddenly, Lucy's orgasmic wail echoes down the stairs. We pan them running to the staircase.

[Upstairs hallway—continuing action]

Steadicam tracking behind them
running to Lucy's door. Lucy's wanton moans repeat again, building to a passionate female climax. Shot continues into Lucy's bedroom—past Van Helsing and Seward to the open window, curtains flapping.

Dracula's shadow
escapes, dripping blood.

[Lucy's bedroom—continuing action]

Low angle
Lucy, in foreground, lies sprawled on her bed, a small pool of blood caking on a pillow. Her gown is torn open to her waist. Van Helsing covers her.

VAN HELSING
She's only a child!

Lucy's chest heaves, struggling to breathe. He checks her pulse, her jugular. The choker hinders him. He slides it down—

Van Helsing's POV
revealing the two small punctures. We track in close to the wounds. Fresh. Larger.

Worn with repeated use.

VAN HELSING
Oh, my God.

Low angle closeup—Van Helsing
His expression tells all. He knows. He knows!

VAN HELSING
There is no time to be lost. There must be transfusion at once.

Close on Van Helsing's bag
as he pulls out implements. Pull back to two-shot of Seward and Van Helsing preparing for transfusion.

VAN HELSING
You still remember how to tie a tourniquet, don't you, Jack? Take off your coat.

AN AGE OF WONDERS

"There are no limits to science," Dracula marvels, upon first viewing the miracle of cinema. The late Victorian age, when *Dracula* is set, was a period of great technological innovation, a time when science and rationality clashed with tradition and faith. Stoker dramatizes this encounter in his novel, and Coppola has emphasized it.

Mina's typewriter and shorthand, Jack Seward's cylinder recorder and psychological researches, the cinema itself, and the primitive transfusions performed to save Lucy—all show Stoker's keen interest in scientific progress. Seeking new images to "shake up the audience," Coppola once considered replacing the coach that brings Harker to Castle Dracula with "some kind of incredible touring car."

Blood typing was not discovered until 1912, so transfusions attempted before then were highly risky. Sometimes it worked and sometimes it didn't; doctors didn't know why.

This mystery extends the symbolic meaning of blood in the Dracula story.

Blood is the source of all life and the "sauce of all passion," as Coppola notes. But in vampire tales, it is also an unholy sacrament (as when Dracula shares blood with Mina and calls her his bride) and the medium of a dread disease. The similarity between vampirism and AIDS, both connected with blood and sexuality, did not go unnoticed by the *Dracula* filmmakers.

"Van Helsing represents the scientific mind of his day," notes Francis Coppola. Part Sherlock Holmes and part Sigmund Freud, Van Helsing uses his powerful intellect to unravel clues and look into minds and hearts. Yet he is not bound by the rational; he respects the supernatural, the unexplainable. As he tells Seward, "You do not let your eyes see nor your ears hear that which you cannot account for. . . There are always mysteries in life."

Performing the transfusion on Lucy.

The young men walk outside to clear their heads and debate the mystery of Lucy's illness.

SEWARD
You've perfected the procedure?

VAN HELSING
Perfected? No. I've only experimented. Landsteiner's method. Animals, goats, sheeps. . . .

SEWARD
And what if hemolysis occurs in the blood donor serum?

VAN HELSING
Her red blood cells will explode.

View on door
Holmwood, in his hat and topcoat, bursts in.

HOLMWOOD
What in God's name is going on here?!

He grabs at Van Helsing. Seward pulls him back. Van Helsing looks at Seward, then at Holmwood.

SEWARD
This is Professor Van Helsing, Art.

HOLMWOOD
What the hell is he doing to Lucy!

SEWARD
He's trying to save her life!

Medium close shot Van Helsing

VAN HELSING
Ah, the fiancé. You've come in time. This young lady is very ill. She wants blood, and blood she must have. Take off your coat. Roll up your sleeve—quickly, quickly!

He holds up two ghastly needles in each hand, connected by tubing and a bulb pump.

SEWARD
This may hurt a little, Art.

Wide four-shot

Seward sits Holmwood down, ties off his arm with a jealous jerk, and thumps up a vein. He jabs Holmwood with one large needle, as Van Helsing inserts the other into

Lucy's arm. She quivers in brief pain—still unconscious.

Close shot
The needle in Holmwood.

View on Holmwood

HOLMWOOD
Forgive me, sir. My life is hers. I would give my last drop of blood to save her.

VAN HELSING
Really? How interesting. I do not ask as much as that, yet.

Extreme closeup
Blood traveling in the tube; feeding life into Lucy.

Closeup
A thin stream of blood falling from the apparatus and pooling on a glass slide below.

Cut to:
[*Hillingham garden—night*]

Pan with suitors
as they exit the house. Holmwood totes brandy and a snifter. Quincey is dazed. Seward toys with his lancet nervously.

HOLMWOOD
Jack, that poor creature has had put into her veins the blood of two men in as many days.

QUINCEY
Man alive, her whole body wouldn't hold that much blood.
(*sits on a bench*)
What took it out?

VAN HELSING
Good question, Mr. Morris.

Van Helsing startles them from the shadows. Seward nearly stabs himself with his lancet. Van Helsing lights his cigar. We track in on Seward as he approaches.

SEWARD
Those marks on her throat. No disease. No trituration. I'm sure the blood loss occurred there.

VAN HELSING
Oh? Where did the blood go? You were once a careful student, Jack. Use your brain. Where did the blood go? Tell me!

GARDEN AND MAZE

The garden set, showing the fountain and maze.

The garden at Hillingham estate was built on Stage 30 of the old MGM lot (now Sony Studios), which holds the famous "Esther Williams tank," an enormous concrete-lined pool. This enabled the *Dracula* art department to create an entire English sunken garden, with a reflecting pool, a maze, a family cemetery modeled loosely on London's Highgate Cemetery, and the striking entrance to the Westenra family crypt.

"Working on sound stages made it easy to control the interiors," says production designer Tom Sanders, "but for exteriors it can be very frightening. You need to feel that you are outside, so the matte paintings and all the green tones and the textures and lighting have to work together just right. Duplicating nature is tough."

The maze, a key feature of the set, was partly constructed and partly painted on a backing to add several hundred feet of depth. During a scene where characters run through the maze, the hedges are moved just ahead of the camera, "so we ended up with an endless amount of maze from 30 feet of hedge," recalls Sanders.

The garden was part of a larger set that also depicted several rooms of the house: the front portico exterior, foyer, living room, and conservatory. "It was really 3 or 4 sets combined into one," notes Sanders. "They could film through one part into another, or out into the garden, and create a real sense of depth that way."

Closeup Seward
feeling the fool.

SEWARD
The bedclothes would be covered in blood.

Closeup Van Helsing

VAN HELSING
Exactly. You do not let your eyes see nor
your ears hear that which you cannot
account for.

Over Van Helsing on Seward and Quincey
Van Helsing stalks Seward and Quincey
back.

SEWARD
(frustrated)
Something just went up there, sucked it out
of her, and flew away, I suppose?

*Van Helsing plays
hide-and-seek in the
dark garden to make a
Socratic point.*

Closeup Van Helsing

VAN HELSING
Ja. Why not?

Medium wide three-shot
Van Helsing is relentless, goading Seward to
a trembling mess. Holmwood empties his
snifter, woozy and pissed.

HOLMWOOD
That's it, is it?
(shakes his head in disgust)
That's brilliant. That's absolutely brilliant.
Will one of you learned doctors, or whatever you are, kindly tell me what is going on
with my Lucy!

VAN HELSING
(ignores him)
Jack, you are a scientist. Do you not think
there are things in this universe which you
cannot understand—and yet which are true?

He gestures to the starry night above.

SEWARD
You know I do not.

Both men speak at the same time, alternat-
ing in closeup.

VAN HELSING
(relentless)
Mesmerism? Hypnotism? Electromagnetic
fields?

SEWARD
(conceding)
You and Charcot have proved hypnotism.

Van Helsing turns away and dramatically
faces the graveyard and gardens in the darkness. We push in past Seward on Van Helsing's back.

VAN HELSING
Astral bodies . . . Materialization?

On Seward and Holmwood
Seward turns angrily to confront Van Helsing—

Their POV:
He's gone. Vanished into thin air! We track
back and pan to include the men as Van
Helsing suddenly steps out from behind a
tree—

94

VAN HELSING
See?

On Seward

SEWARD
I feel like a blundering novice.

Closeup Van Helsing
Dead serious. Proclaiming the truth.

VAN HELSING
Gentlemen! We're not fighting a disease here. Those marks on your dear Miss Lucy's neck were made by something unspeakable out there. Dead but not dead. It stalks us, for some dread purpose I do not yet comprehend.

The garden is suddenly a very uninviting place to the men.

VAN HELSING
Believe! It feeds on Lucy's precious blood. It is a beast . . . a monster.

The winds rise.

Dissolve to:
[Carfax—night]

Closeup Dracula
resting in his box. Wet lips red with life.

Hunger sated. Rivulets of blood flow from his mouth.

Insert—Carfax exterior, in long shot and medium shot

Dissolve to:
[Hillingham—day]

Closeup—face of Mina
in a mirror, at her vanity. We slowly pull back.

MINA (V.O.)
"Diary again. . . . Lucy has had another setback. I loathe to see her pain. . . . Forgive me, my Jonathan, in your absence I must confess; I long to see the stranger with eyes like burning flames."

During voiceover, scene shifts to Lucy's bedroom as she sleeps; Mina nursing her, clearing an untouched tray of food away. Dracula watches them both from outside the window. (Music cue.)

Extreme closeup
Mina's eye

Dissolve to:

Overhead shot
Top of absinthe glass

Envisioning the place where Dracula would take Mina for their first real "date," screenwriter Jim Hart said, "I'm thinking of a restaurant that would be inhabited by the artists of the day, like Oscar Wilde . . . the equivalent of a coffeehouse in the sixties. A place where Mina would never go, but Dracula would love it because it's populated by all these artistic, bohemian types."

The film restaurant was Rule's Cafe, and its bohemian denizens of the *fin de siècle* would have favored a potent, pale green liqueur called absinthe. Concocted from wormwood and various herbs, absinthe has an anise flavor and a very high alcohol content; consumed in sufficient quantity, it causes hallucinations and addiction. Oscar Wilde once rhapsodized, "A glass of absinthe is the most poetical thing in the world."

Absinthe was consumed in vast quantities by Symbolist poets such as Verlaine and Rimbaud and its effects shockingly depicted by post-Impressionist painters including Manet, Degas, and the early Picasso. It came to be regarded in France as such a plague that by 1914 temperance zealots managed to have it banned.

"Absinthe was sort of the LSD of the Victorian era," Francis Coppola told his production team, "and it was known as the Green Fairy. Like a sexy woman who got into your brain. That's the kind of drugged, decadent Oscar Wilde level that Jim Hart has tried to lay into the script; it's the spirit of Rule's Cafe. . . . It enables our entire storytelling method to be a kind of Symbolist trance."

[Rule's Cafe—private dining room—night]

Closeup—glass
A bottle of water comes into view. A hand pours the water over a sugar cube on silver apparatus into a glass of absinthe, turning the absinthe a milky green.

DRACULA (O.S.)
Absinthe is the aphrodisiac of the self. The "green fairy" who lives in the absinthe wants your soul. But . . . you are safe with me.

We pan to closeup on Mina's hand, picking up sugar cube and carrying it slowly to her lips. She sucks it erotically.

MINA
Tell me, Prince . . . tell me of your home.

Closeup Dracula

DRACULA
The most beautiful place in all creation.

Extreme closeup
His blue eye, cut to Mina's brown one.

Closeup Mina
Her eyes faraway, intoxicated. Her hair worn down for the first time, as in the mosaic portrait of Elizabeth.

MINA
Yes . . . it must be. A land beyond a great vast forest . . . surrounded by majestic mountains . . . lush vineyards, with flowers of such frailty and beauty as to be found nowhere else—

Dracula's hand with its crested ring crosses before his face in closeup.

Close on Mina's profile
Dracula enters frame close to her.

DRACULA
You describe my home as if you . . . had seen it firsthand. . . .

MINA
It is your voice, perhaps. It is so . . . familiar . . . like a voice in a dream I cannot place. . . It comforts me . . . when I am alone.

Their eyes meet, both lingering too long. He caresses her neck—she lets him. Then she rises, moves out of frame. We stay on Dracula.

MINA
And what of the princess?

DRACULA
Princess?

Past Dracula to Mina
She looks out into the main room.

MINA
There is always a princess—gowns flowing white, her face a . . .
(lost in hallucination)
. . . a river.

Insert:
Elizabeth falling past the castle walls.

MINA
The princess is a river filled with tears of sadness and heartbreak.

Single (reverse) on Dracula
turned to her; his reaction to her words.

97

THE "RIVER PRINCESS"

Castle Bran in Transylvania is often mistaken as Dracula's castle, and conveys the legacy of his times.

Screenwriter Jim Hart came upon a fascinating tale concerning the death of the Dracula's first wife (who is unnamed in the historical chronicles). In 1462, Dracula's forces were being hard-pressed by the advancing Turks—in fact, this was to be the last year of his second reign, followed by twelve years of imprisonment.

Dracula, his family, and a few faithful followers took refuge in his mountain retreat on the Arges River. Castle Dracula is located at the souce of the river, where it tumbles in a torrent out of the Carpathians. The site was inaccessible and well fortified; the Turks bombarded it with cannon fire but with little success.

A final assault was planned. The night before, according to stories passed down by peasants of the region, a Romanian slave in the Turkish army climbed a bluff across the river from the castle and fired an arrow across the narrow gorge into a window. The arrow, bearing a message warning Dracula to escape while he could, was found by his wife, who brought it to her husband and told him that she would rather be eaten by the fish of the Arges than fall into the hands of the Turks. Before anyone could stop her, she ran up the stairs to the topmost tower and hurled herself into the rushing stream.

In another version of the tale—the one used in the film—Dracula is away at battle, and the message falsely informs his lady that he has been killed, precipitating her suicide.

The river water still flows with a red cast in that place—not, as local folklore claims, from the princess's blood, but because red bricks from the ruined castle have fallen there. But for many years, that spot has been known as Riul Doamei, "the Princess's river."

Mina is lost in the absinthe dream, trying to decipher sensations surging through her.

Back to Dracula
He gets up, and we pan and track him to a close two-shot with Mina; his arms hold her.

DRACULA
There was a Princess, Elizabeta. *(speaking "Elizabeta" as if it were Mina's given name)*

She was the most radiant woman of all the empires of the world. Man's deceit took her from her ancient prince. She leapt to her death into the river you spoke of. . . . In my mother tongue it is called Arges—"River Princess."

Closeup
Mina's tearstreaked face. He gently gathers a tear on his index finger, quickly closes his hand. Then opens it, revealing several sparkling diamonds. Mina smiles through her tears. He kisses her tenderly, passionately.

Dissolve to:
[Rule's Cafe/Castle Dracula—night]
Three-sixty-degree tracking shot around Mina and Dracula, waltzing. Hundreds of candles flicker in the dark background. With each turn, Dracula becomes more fluid and comfortable in Mina's arms and

---

Costume designer Eiko Ishioka:

"Throughout the film, red is highly significant as the color that symbolizes blood. Therefore I decided to use red only for Dracula. The only exception was for the dress that Mina wears when she dances with Dracula on their 'first date.' This was a dress Dracula had made especially for her, the object of his passionate love, so for this dress he chose his theme color— suggesting that Mina soon will become a vampire."

Harker, in desperate straits, arrives at the convent.

she in his. She is awakening his dead soul.

As they are dancing, the lights on the walls slowly come up to reveal Harker, running down the castle stairs carrying two impalement stakes from the crypt, fashioned into a huge crucifix. The Brides pursue him. At the bottom of the stairs, he turns, lowering the crucifix like a lance, jabbing at them, keeping them at bay like wolves. They retreat.

HARKER (V.O.)
"I shall not remain alone with these awful women; I shall try to scale the castle wall farther than I have yet attempted."

[Castle wall and precipice—later]

View on the window
(Music cue.) The Arges River roars far below. Harker (clothed) comes into frame and descends the stone wall; slipping, clinging, cutting himself.

HARKER (V.O.)
"I may find a way from this dreadful place. And then away for home! Away to the quickest and nearest train! Away from this cursed spot, from this cursed land, where the devil and his children still walk with earthly feet!"

"At least God's mercy is better than that of these monsters, and the precipice is steep and high. At its foot a man may sleep—as a man. Good-bye, all! Good-bye, Mina!"

His bloody fingers give way. He skids down the face—

Dissolve to:
[Carpathian woods—night]

Close on Harker
crawling. (Music cue: howling wind.)

Wider shot
We are on his back as he climbs up a hill through a rush of mud and rain, drowning, sinking, dying. The camera tilts up, comes over the edge of the hill. Through the rain Harker sees a cross! Glowing; it's a window! A door!

He stumbles toward the convent, where he pound on the door and finds refuge.

Fade out. Fade in:

[Hillingham—day]

Steadicam shot
Mina is in the garden maze, breathless, reading a letter. She trembles visibly.

MINA
Jonathan is alive. He's alive.

We track in front of her as she begins to run through the garden, her excitement building, beside herself. Her joy melts to anguish and heartbreak. She stops into a closeup in the gazebo.

MINA
My sweet prince—Jonathan must never know of us.

She exits frame right.

Bottom of stairs
We track on Mina's back as she runs up the steps, pulling herself together, closing the door on Dracula forever.

MINA
Lucy! Lucy— Oh.

We move up the steps and discover Van Helsing and Seward with Mina, ending in an over shoulder Mina on the men.

VAN HELSING
Abraham Van Helsing.

MINA
(has heard talk of him)
Dr. Van Helsing.

VAN HELSING
Ah, you are Madam Mina, dear friend to our Lucy.

MINA
How is she, Doctor?

VAN HELSING
She is still very weak. She tells me of your beloved Jonathan Harker and your worry for him. I too worry—for all young lovers.

Over Van Helsing on Mina
He suddenly starts waltzing with her, singing.

Letter, Sister Agatha, Hospital of St. Joseph and Ste. Mary, Buda-Pesth, to Miss Wilhelmina Murray.

"12 August.

"Dear Madam,—
I write by desire of Mr. Jonathan Harker, who is not strong enough to write, though progressing well, thanks to God and St. Joseph and Ste. Mary. He has been under our care for nearly six weeks, suffering from a violent brain fever. . . . He will require some few weeks' rest in our sanatorium in the hills, but will then return. . . .

"Believe me,
Yours, with sympathy and all blessings,
"Sister Agatha.

"P.S. —My patient being asleep, I open this to let you know something more. He has told me all about you, and that you are shortly to be his wife. All blessings to you both! He has had some fearful shock—so says our doctor—and in his delirium his ravings have been dreadful; of wolves and poison and blood; of ghosts and demons; and I fear to say of what. Be careful with him always that there may be nothing to excite him of this kind for a long time to come. . . . He came in the train from Klausenberg, and the guard was told by the station-master there that he rushed into the station shouting for a ticket home. Seeing from his violent demeanour that he was English, they gave him a ticket for the furthest station on the way thither that the train reached. . . ."

Single on Seward
His reaction.

Back to over Van Helsing on Mina
He stops and looks directly into her eyes.

VAN HELSING
There are darknesses in life, and there are lights. You are one of the lights, dear Mina. The light of all lights. Go now—see your friend.

Mina exits frame and enters Lucy's room through terrace doors. We stay on Van Helsing, watching her go.

[Lucy's bedroom—day]

Medium wide shot—Lucy
Sleeping. She has a look of death about her.

A vase of white flowers is on the table next to her bed. Mina enters frame into two-shot, about to burst in spite of her shock at Lucy's degenerative state. She takes Lucy's hand—Lucy stirs awake. Camera moves in on Lucy .

LUCY
Mina? You're different. You look positively radiant. You heard from Jonathan—didn't you?

Closeup—on Mina over Lucy
Lucy hugs Mina with failing arms. Van Helsing and Seward enter through terrace door in background. Van Helsing moves to a chair; Seward stays at the doorway.

MINA
Yes—he's safe, Lucy. He's in a convent in Roumania, suffering from a violent brain fever. The good sisters caring for him—

MAKING MEMORIES AT "CAMP COPPOLA"

Soon after casting on *Dracula* was completed, the principals began rehearsals, first gathering for a week at the Coppola ranch/winery in California's Napa Valley. Francis Coppola's teenage experience as a drama camp counselor taught the filmmaker valuable lessons about giving a disparate group of young actors common ground to work from.

"The first thing you want," he says, "is just a chance to be with the cast without any other element poking its nose in. You want them to

The director makes a point to Keanu Reeves.

get to know each other in the most creative way." At "Camp Coppola" there were balloon and horseback rides for Elwes, Campbell, Grant, and Reeves; mass dinners at a long table on the porch; theater games and improvisations. The actors read the entire novel aloud, staged scenes from the script, and offered notes on their parts.

"Francis embraces you like you're his family," says Gary Oldman. "He brought us all together as an ensemble. You rarely have rehearsal in movies, and it's a luxury." Richard E. Grant adds: "By the time we started shooting, I knew exactly what character I was playing and who I was in relation to everybody else."

Associate producer Susie Landau notes, "One reason for rehearsing in Napa was to take everybody out of their usual contexts . . . a step to breaking down their barriers. Much as in a theater company, a trust developed and a true feeling of ensemble emerged."

The cast also assembled for a staged reading of the script by radio actors at a cabaret near the American Zoetrope headquarters in San Francisco. Just before filming began, they met again for two weeks of rehearsals at Hollywood's United Methodist Church, a famed practice venue—"like a Broadway show rehearsing in Boston," says Landau. These sessions, complete with lighting and sound, were videotaped and the footage incorporated into Coppola's electronic storyboard.

Coppola observes that "for most actors, there's some simple little experience, some barrier they have to overcome, and on the other side they're home free with their character. I try to let them have that experience as soon as possible."

they wrote to me, they say he needs me. . . .
But I must stay with you—

Higher angle
looking down on Lucy over Mina. Lucy
looks Mina squarely in the eye, her breathing shorter, desperate. We slowly track in
to a closeup of Lucy .

LUCY
Mina—go to him, love him and marry him
right then and there. Don't waste another
precious moment of life without each
other. . . .

Single on Van Helsing
in a chair, observing.

50/50 shot—the two girls
We track in, favoring Lucy.

LUCY
I want you to take this, my sister . . . my
wedding gift to you . . . take it . . .

She discreetly slides her engagement ring
off her bony finger and curls it in Mina's
hand.

Close shot—the jewelry
Lucy's hands giving it to Mina.

Closeup Mina
She is overwhelmed. She shakes her head
"no" repeatedly.

LUCY (O.S.)
Bad luck if you say no. Don't worry yourself about spoiled little Lucy. I'll be all right.

Medium wide shot

LUCY
(clasping Mina's hands)
Tell Jonathan . . . oceans of love . . .

MINA
(finishing)
. . . millions of kisses.

Mina kisses her, and arranges the vase of
flowers by Lucy's bed. Lucy suddenly shrieks.

LUCY
Is this why I cannot breathe!?

She shatters the vase. We track in fast as
Van Helsing and Seward enter frame, hurrying to Lucy, into a tight shot on Lucy
over the men. They try to subdue her.

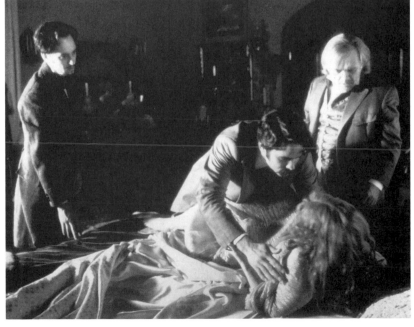

Dr. Seward's Diary

11 September.—This afternoon I went over to Hillingham. Found Van Helsing in excellent spirits, and Lucy much better. Shortly after I had arrived, a big parcel from abroad came for the Professor. . . . a great bundle of white flowers.

"These are for you, Miss Lucy," he said. . . . "There is much virtue in these so common flower. See, I place them myself in your room, I make myself the wreath that you are to wear. . . . Now sit still awhile. Come with me, friend John, and you shall help me deck the room with garlic, which is all the way from Haarlem, where my friend Vanderpool raise herb in his glass-houses all the year. I had to telegraph yesterday, or they would not have been here."

We went into the room, taking the flowers with us. The Professor's actions were certainly odd and not to be found in any pharmacopoeia that I ever heard of. First he fastened up the windows and latched them securely; next, taking a handful of the flowers, he rubbed them all over the sashes; as though to ensure that every whiff of air that might get in would be laden with the garlic smell. Then with the wisp he rubbed all over the jamb of the door, above, below, and at each side, and round the fireplace in the same way. It all seemed grotesque to me. . . .

VAN HELSING
It is medicinal—so that you may sleep well—and dream pleasant—

Lucy tears the flower necklace off.

LUCY
Garlic! These flowers are common garlic!

She struggles, writhing, crying out. Quincey enters—Seward tries to distract Lucy.

SEWARD
Lucy—look, here's Quincey! Quincey's here to see you!
(to Mina)
Brandy—get some brandy.

Mina exits.

Low angle (Lucy's POV) on Quincey
Quincey is shocked by Lucy's appearance, but puts on his big grin.

QUINCEY
Miss Lucy, you just rest easy. Art sent me to take care of you. He said if you don't get better right quick, I'll have to put you out of your misery like a lame horse.

Over Quincey on Lucy
Lucy, seeing Quincey, brightens like her old tart self; her laugh tinkling like those of the vampire brides. She gets more and more provocative. Van Helsing observes intently.

LUCY
Oh, Quincey, you're such a beast. Will you kiss me—kiss me once more—

Her voice is soft, voluptuous, reeking with desire. Quincey bends to her, eager—Van Helsing explodes, catching Quincey with a fury, yanking him back across the room—

VAN HELSING
Not for your life! Or hers!

Low angle—on Van Helsing and Seward
Lucy swoons. Van Helsing waves Quincey out and hovers over her, checking her vitals, her receding gums. We move in on him.

VAN HELSING
Look! *Ja . . . nosferatu . . . ja.*

Insert:
A 15th-century woodcut of Dracula, seated at a feast, tears in his eyes, witnessing mass impalement. We track in on the drawing.

Dissolve to:
[Rule's main room—night]

Wide shot
Dracula sitting alone at a table set with an elegant meal for two. The maitre d'hotel gives him a letter. He opens it, reads.

MINA (V.O.)
"My dearest Prince—forgive me."

We track in to a closeup of Dracula. Tears in his eyes; each word wrenching him like a wild animal caught in a trap.

MINA (V.O. CONTINUED)
"I have received word from my fiancé in Roumania . . . ."

Close shot—the letter
Tears drop, blurring the ink. They are Dracula's! We move in on the page.

Close shot—splat
Purple ink. It becomes, as we dissolve to:

[Ocean—night]

Purple sea—the wake of a boat
moving away. We see a page of diary hitting the water and drifting away. We tilt up to see the page flying away into the ocean.

Medium wide shot—Mina
standing on the boat. We track in a little closer and see her methodically tearing out pages and throwing them overboard, watching each memory drift away.

MINA (V.O. CONTINUED)
"I am en route to join him. We are to be married. I will never see you again. Mina. . . ."

She starts to toss his single white kid glove, touching it to her face. Tears finally come. Her inner strength failing, she sobs, closing the door on Dracula . . . forever. . . .

Left: *Woodcut from a German pamphlet about Dracula, published in Nuremberg in 1499.* Below: *Dracula receives Mina's note.*

Close shot
The white glove is borne away by the waves.

[Rule's Cafe/Castle courtyard—night]

Resume: closeup Dracula (his back)
We slowly track around. Head in hands, fighting his grief, hiding his tears. Kid gloves stained with blood! He removes them, revealing the face of the Old Dracula. The animal/wolf that rules him is suggested in his features— wolfen—demonic! He jumps up.

High angle shot
looking down at Dracula. He roars in the center of the dark courtyard in all his hideous glory, summoning the forces of hell. Hundreds of candles around him.

DRACULA
(*metallic, from the grave*)
Winds! Windsss!!

Then the camera flies up and the candles blow out.

Dissolve to:
[Hillingham—night]

Wide low angle
(Music cue.) Van Helsing's coach arrives. It is extremely windy. Van Helsing is shouting something inside.

Van Helsing
We pan him over from the coach to Seward

and Quincey. We see the wind blowing their coats. Van Helsing is in a state of near-hysterical excitement.

VAN HELSING
Jack, hurry, man. I have much to tell you. Guard her well, Mr. Morris, do not fail here tonight. We are dealing with forces beyond all human experience. . . an enormous power.
(laughing)
So guard her well! Otherwise your precious Lucy may become a bitch of the devil.

Medium closeup Quincey
Disgusted, ready to punch Van Helsing out.

QUINCEY
You're a sick old buzzard—

Two-shot Van Helsing and Quincey

VAN HELSING
Hear me out, young man. Lucy is not a random victim attacked by mere accident, you understand me? No—she is a willing recruit, a follower, I daresay—a devoted disciple. She is the devil's concubine.

Quincey looks to Seward for explanation of this nonsense.

VAN HELSING
We may yet save her precious soul . . .
(laughs maniacally)
But not on an empty stomach. Jack! I starve!

We pan Seward and Van Helsing to the

Opposite: *Mina en route to join Harker, and pages from her typed diary.* Above: *Dracula summons the winds.*

coach. It speeds away, leaving Quincey behind.

Close on Quincey's rifle
He checks it. We tilt up to his face, checking the sky.

Insert:
Closeup of pistol case; a hand lifts out one of the weapons; loads it.

From Francis Coppola's journal:

"The Lucy part is the most flamboyantly erotic, combining acting with beauty. She has to be young, no older than 22, because she'll be working opposite Mina, as her contemporary. Whoever we cast has to decide that she's prepared to do what we need. Nudity isn't the issue; it's the attitude, the intensity it takes to say, 'I'm going to do something really dazzling.' She has to be really brave."

[Carfax—night]
Dracula's pixilation POV
from gardens at Carfax, through maze, into creatures, etc.

[Lucy's bedroom—night]
High angle
Holmwood sits vigil with Lucy, who appears near death. Camera booms down. Holmwood downs a Scotch, then another. He aims the pistol at imaginary targets around the room.

[Hillingham grounds]
High angle
looking down at Quincey from Lucy's terrace as he patrols, watching the evil sky. He hears howling! The wind? Dogs? Closer! A wolf? He looks up at the sky.

Quincey's POV—the sky
The clouds are frightening, forming into shapes.

Medium closeup—Quincey
He cocks his rifle.

[Hillingham grounds—night]

Pixilation POV
continues, coming closer. It kills an estate watchman.

[Lucy's bedroom]

Her eyes snap open.

[Convent chapel—night]

Long lens shot—a tall gold crucifix
against the chapel window, beams of light breaking through as the cross moves toward the altar, carried by a priest. A nuns' choir chants God's praises. Harker and Mina are about to be married.

[Lucy's bedroom]

Medium high angle
Holmwood nods off in the chair beside Lucy.

Close shot
His hand goes limp at his side, dropping the empty shot glass. Winds lash the windows.

[Hillingham grounds]

Dracula's pixilation POV—approaching Quincey
The view jumps to his rifle, then jumps to his gleaming knife. Quincey turns, sensing the presence—view rushes closer. He aims at the camera and fires!

[Lucy's bedroom]

She senses Dracula's presence approaching nearer, bares her fangs, pulls the garlic away from her neck.

[Convent chapel—night]

Harker and Mina stand before the altar. Priest blesses the couple, places wreaths on their heads.

[Hillingham grounds]

The view comes closer to Quincey. We see the terrifying form of Dracula as the wolf-beast, rushing up the steps, knocking Quincey to the ground.

Quincey's POV—a shadowy figure
with red eyes rears on its hind legs and charges upright over him!

Dracula's pixilation POV
continues up the steps, approaching Lucy's window. We see rats, vermin, birds falling.

[Lucy's bedroom—continuing action]

Two-shot master
Lucy's head leaning back over the bed. We see her body, the window at an angle over her, Dracula in it, looking at her. No longer the handsome creature of desire, but the horrible old man.

Closeup Lucy
We slowly pull back from her in a high

Opposite: *Holmwood guards his fiancée.* Above: *Lucy aroused and showing her nascent fangs.*

109

Opposite: *Dracula commands Lucy from the window.* This page: *Van Helsing orders Quincey to stand watch, but he cannot thwart Dracula's final and fatal attack on Lucy.*

111

Mina and Jonathan are married . . .

angle shot as she gets ready for Dracula; we see her hunger.

View on Holmwood
He wakes in a daze, disoriented. He looks to Lucy, confused.

Lucy's POV—balcony door
Medium closeup of the demonic Dracula looking at her.

He gestures—sending a startled Holmwood crashing against the wall, knocking him unconscious.

DRACULA
(*to Lucy*)
Your impotent men with their foolish spells cannot protect you from my power—

Resume: Chapel wedding

Closeup Harker
Drinks the wedding sacrament from a chalice.

Resume: Dracula and Lucy

DRACULA
I condemn you to living death—to eternal hunger for living blood—

[Lucy's bedroom—continuing action]

Dracula raises his arms, calling forth a tempest. The wolf leaps right through him (optical fx or magic mirror fx) as if he were a ghost—

Close on Lucy
Her hand glides to the garland around her neck—and rips it away, revealing her neck and throat—she pulls the wolf's head to her.

Resume: Chapel wedding

Mina and Harker
Harker lifts Mina's veil and they kiss. There is hope in Harker's face . . . and in Mina's. Rapid intercut of the kiss, growing more erotic, with the wolf Dracula ravaging Lucy.

. . . as Lucy is mourned.

Fade out. Fade in:

[Hillingham main room—day]

Closeup, pulling back to high overhead angle looking down on Lucy, lovelier than ever. We pull back to reveal that she is surrounded by white satin in a glass coffin. We see Holmwood and Quincey, in tears, behind the head of the coffin. Seward is at the foot. He turns, and we pan with him as he walks to Van Helsing, into a two-shot.

On Van Helsing over Seward

VAN HELSING
You loved her deeply and that is why you must trust me and believe—

On Seward over Van Helsing

SEWARD
(maddened, overwrought)
Believe? How can I believe . . . ?

On Holmwood and Quincey annoyed by the disturbance.

HOLMWOOD
Shhh!

Back to Van Helsing

VAN HELSING
(sotto voce)
I want you to bring me, before night, a set of post-mortem knives.

SEWARD
An autopsy? Lucy?—

VAN HELSING
(matter-of-fact)
Not exactly. I want to cut off her head and take out her heart.

113

Act III

She Is "Vampyre"

London, September 1897

[London street—night—fog]

Wide shot
Camera cranes down as Mina and Harker exit the Victoria train station entrance. People coming and going, porters loading bags into hansoms. Mina is dressed in mourning.

MINA (V.O.)
"Diary, 17th September. Arrived from the continent. This is a sad homecoming in every way. Lucy is gone, never to return to us. Jonathan is only a wreck of himself and still suffers from his malady. He gave me his journal, saying there should be no secrets between husband and wife. I have thus read the terrible record of his ordeal. Jonathan, how can I ever tell you the truth about *my* secrets. . . ."

[Hansom—night]

Medium two-shot
Mina and Harker enter a hansom cab.

[London street—night]

Dracula's pixilation POV
through crowd, building tension, ending in close two-shot of Mina and Harker through the hansom window.

DRACULA (O.S.)
(angry animal whisper)
She belongs to me—

We see Harker turn and react, sensing Dracula's presence.

Harker's POV—Dracula
(Music cue.) Standing full view in the light of the streetlamps, looking right at Harker!

Storyboard art, Harker and Mina's homecoming, as he sees Dracula outside the train station.

116

Younger than Harker remembers him.

[Hansom window—continuing action]

Harker stands; his legs buckle. Mina catches him, cradling him down. His eyes wild in terror and amazement.

MINA
Jonathan? What is it?

HARKER
It is the man himself! He has grown young!

[Hillingham cemetery—night]

Low angle tracking shot (maze)
with the feet of men approaching the crypt. Fog rolls in.

Medium close shot
Lamps flash across the iron gate leading to the family crypt. Holmwood reluctantly unlocks the gate. Van Helsing leads them in.

[Crypt—night]

High wide angle
The men enter. It is very cold. The coffin sits on a stone altar. Seward and Quincey inspect it with their lamps.

HOLMWOOD
Must we desecrate poor Lucy's grave? She died horribly enough—

Medium closeup Van Helsing

VAN HELSING
(a class lecture)
If—Miss Lucy is dead—there can be no wrong done to her. But if she is not—

HOLMWOOD
My God, what are you saying—has she been buried alive?

VAN HELSING
All I say is that she is "un-dead."

The Vampire Killers make their grim pilgrimage to Lucy's crypt.

117

Van Helsing: "I swear to you by all that I hold sacred that I have not removed nor touched her."

Two-shot Seward and Quincey
unscrewing the top of the coffin.

Medium closeup Holmwood
He is an emotional mess.

HOLMWOOD
This is insanity.

Overhead shot
looking down on coffin. Van Helsing pries the lead flange back. As Quincey and Seward remove the lid, the camera pulls slowly back so that when they open it, we see a wide shot of the empty coffin.

Past Van Helsing on Holmwood

HOLMWOOD
Where is she?

He pulls out a pistol, leveling it at Van Helsing.

HOLMWOOD
(screams)
Where is she! What have you done with her?

Over pistol on Van Helsing

VAN HELSING
(calm)
She lives beyond the grace of God. A wanderer in the outer darkness. She is "Vampyre." "Nosferatu." These creatures do not die like the bee after the first sting—but instead grow strong and become immortal once infected by another "nosferatu."
(pushes pistol aside)
So, my friends, we fight not one beast—but legions, that go on age after age, feeding on the blood of the living.

Soft feminine singing drifts into the vault. Holmwood recognizes the voice. He shrinks back—Van Helsing signals. Seward shuts off the lantern.

Wide shot
The men hide near a side wall.

Men's POV—Lucy
in her bridal gown, descending the stairs.

118

She holds a young child at her breast, singing a lullaby, swaying—

View on the men
They react. Holmwood openly gasps.

Back to men's POV of Lucy
We pan her to the coffin. Van Helsing steps out, flanked by the others, and calls to her.

Medium shot Lucy
She turns, and we see her feeding on the child, her lips and gown fresh with a tiny stream of blood. She sees the men, drops the child carelessly to the ground, and steps back.

View on men
Their horrified reaction.

Medium shot child
on the ground. It moans, crying. Seward enters frame, picks it up—checking its condition.

Two-shot—Holmwood and Quincey
Holmwood buckles. Quincey is horrified and aroused at the same time but ready with his rifle—

Tracking with Lucy
She transforms to the beautiful, virginal Lucy. She approaches Holmwood with a voluptuous grace.

LUCY
Come to me, Arthur. Leave these others and come to me. My arms are hungry for you. Come, and we can rest together. Come, my husband, come—

Back to Holmwood
approaching her in a trance; we track in front of him a little as he opens his arms—

HOLMWOOD
Lucy—
Van Helsing jumps between them, raising his crucifix—

Medium close Lucy
(Stoker: "She recoiled from it. Her face was shown in the clear burst of moonlight and by the lamp. . . . If ever a face meant death—if looks could kill—we saw it at the moment.")

We track with Van Helsing, forcing Lucy back. Lucy's eyes burn with an unholy light,

Eiko Ishioka on Lucy's death costume:

"The dresses worn by Lucy had to suggest the eccentricity of the role. I referred to Victorian dresses, but the results turned out quite different. Each costume needed to be sexy, unique, and have an aristocratic elegance. Although she is buried in a wedding dress, it does not belong to any style. The Australian frilled lizard was my source of inspiration. Because Lucy turns into a vampire wearing this dress, I wanted to make sure it would look bizarre and haunting after the transformation. Her makeup was part of the effect: Francis said, 'Lucy's new vampire makeup should still be sexy—but in a more vixen, leering, slut kind of way.' "

119

VIXEN TO VAMPIRE

The pivotal role of Lucy Westenra, the wealthy coquette who falls prey to Dracula's charms, was a major casting concern. From more than 500 actresses considered by casting director Victoria Thomas, Coppola chose newcomer Sadie Frost, who makes her American film debut in *Dracula*. She had wanted to read for Lucy in England but heard she wasn't the right type—then, by coincidence, she was in Los Angeles with her husband, actor Gary Kemp, and available to audition for Coppola. "He's such a good communicator," Frost says, "he put me at ease right away."

Lucy is a complex, sometimes confusing character. "I almost feel as if I'm playing three parts: Lucy as femme fatale, as a girl who feels she's losing her mind, and as the possessed bride of Dracula. Lucy is full of life—she wants to experience everything. And that makes her vulnerable. She's looking for something she can't find in any of her suitors."

Born in London, Frost began acting at age 11 in children's film and theater, and at 19 joined Manchester's Royal Exchange Theatre. Her film credits include *The Krays* and *Dark Obsession*. She has also performed extensively in British television.

Frost was trained as a gymnast, which Coppola put to good use. "It meant that she could get into difficult positions and move in an interesting way—which fits, since Dracula's wives are aligned with the animal world." In some of Lucy's scenes—such as when she re-enters her coffin in the crypt—her movements are filmed backwards, producing a weird effect when the film is run forwards. At one time, she practiced slithering down the crypt stairs like a snake, but her elaborate death costume made that impractical.

The scenes where Lucy is sexually aroused by Dracula's presence were nerve-wracking for Frost, but she found a technique that allowed her to enter "a kind of obsessive trance and act those scenes just as movement, a kind of dance."

and she vomits blood on him as she enters her coffin.

[Crypt interior—night]

Quincey and Holmwood
Van Helsing hands Holmwood the stake.

VAN HELSING (O.S.)
A moment's courage and it is done. Take the stake in your left hand, place the point over her heart—and in God name's strike. Do it now!

Roaring his agony, Holmwood strikes. Lucy opens her mouth to scream. Van Helsing enters frame from other side and cuts off her head before she can make a sound. (Music cue.)

[Carfax chapel—night]

Dracula in his coffin, reacts to Lucy's awful demise.

Insert—Lucy's head
rolls away through empty space.

Fade out. Fade in:
[Berkeley hotel grill—day]

Close shot—a table
Harker's journal and Mina's diary rest on a table in the foreground. Food abounds. We see a fork and knife come in and slice off a slab of unusually rare roast beef. Camera tilts up to closeup Van Helsing, carving the slices, regaling the couple with his new discovery. He puts slices of red meat on Mina's plate.

VAN HELSING
Eat! Feast! You will need your strength for the dark days ahead.

Over Van Helsing on Mina and Harker
They sit there, traumatized, petrified.

MINA
Please tell me, Doctor, how did Lucy die? I must know. She was my dearest friend, and no one has told me.

Insert—crypt

"Arthur never faltered. He looked like a figure of Thor as his untrembling arm rose and fell, driving deeper and deeper the mercy-bearing stake."

121

Most movies are "storyboarded"—that is, the director sketches out, shot by shot, his ideas for translating the script to screen, or works with an artist to do so. On *Dracula*, the scope of this process extended far beyond the usual.

"Basically, it's common sense that if you're going to produce a complicated motion picture with thousands of images all organized with actors and costumes and stuff, it's sort of like building a skyscraper," Coppola says. "You need good, detailed plans. The irony is that a lot of films today are really made by the seat of their pants. We wanted to be more efficient and minimize confusion."

The process began with Coppola (aided by researcher Anahid Nazarian) assembling hundreds of "found images" from many sources—books on Symbolist painting, Byzantine decorative arts, and Victorian style; stills from classic films such as Eisenstein's *Ivan the Terrible*—to serve as visual guides to the mood

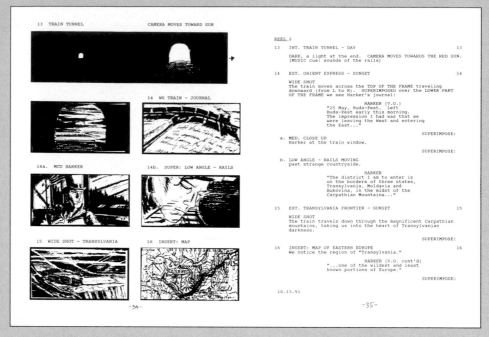

A typical spread from the Dracula *"score."*

and feeling he hoped to create. These images were sequenced and stored in Mavica disk format and later transferred to videotape, with the script read over them.

The next step was to storyboard the entire film, which was done by a team led by Roman Coppola and including sketch artist Peter Ramsay, cinematographer Michael Ballhaus, first assistant director Peter Giuliano, and members of the art department. "We spent several weeks trying to knock the thing down to about a thousand shots that told the story," says the director. When complete, the storyboard drawings were matched with the script page by page to create the "score"—a detailed shooting guide and "the bible of the show."

Again, the drawings

were transferred to tape and the script read as a voiceover. Still later, footage from rehearsals was incorporated as Ballhaus shot them with a Hi8 camera. "I always had a tape I could play that told the whole story," says Coppola. "Some of it was drawings, some from rehearsals, and later, scenes from the actual production, until it became the entire film."

"What the score provided," notes producer Chuck Mulvehill, "was more than a shot list. It enabled us to go on the stage knowing precisely what we wanted. It simplified our lives incredibly."

Production designer Tom Sanders concurs. "The score was a great tool for narrowing everything down, because each storyboard showed the size of the frame that he wanted to shoot the heads in. We always had a reference for how wide and how close—for his thinking, really. We'd look at the score and Francis would say, 'Go ahead and paint the picture behind this.'"

From Sergei Eisenstein's Ivan the Terrible (Part One), *1944.*

High angle wide shot
The men are gathered around Lucy, exhausted. Lucy's head in place, the stake through her heart. They gaze in shame and wonder "as they had seen Lucy in life, with her face of unequaled sweetness and purity." (Stoker)

MINA
Was she in great pain?

Closeup Van Helsing
The rare roast beef big in the foreground (short lens). He is eating and drinking ale.

VAN HELSING
Great pain? *Ja*, she was in great pain.
(pause)
Then we cut her off her head and drove a stake through her heart and burned it—and then she found peace.

Van Helsing laughs, licking his bloody fingers.

Extreme closeup Mina
Mina gasps, horrified.

Mina Harker's Journal

Dr. Van Helsing went on with a sort of cheerfulness which showed that the serious work had begun: "Let us consider the limitations of the vampire in general, and this one in particular.

"For, let me tell you, he is known everywhere that men have been. In old Greece, in old Rome; he flourish in Germany all over, in France, in India, and in China. He have follow in the wake of the berserker Icelander, the devil-begotten Hun, the Slav, the Saxon, the Magyar. . . . The vampire live on, and cannot die by mere passing of time; he can flourish when that he can fatten on the blood of the living. . . . He throws no shadow; he make in the mirror no reflect. . . . He can transform himself to wolf; he can be as bat; he can come in mist, but from what we know, the distance he can make this mist is limited, and it can only be round himself. He come on moonlight rays as dust, as Jonathan saw those sisters in the castle of Dracula. . . . He can see in the dark—no small power, this, in a world which is one half shut from the light. . . . He can do all these things, yet he is not free; he who is not of nature has yet to obey some of nature's laws—why we know not. He may not enter anywhere unless there be someone of the household who bid him to come; though afterwards he can come as he please. His power ceases, as does that of all evil things, at the coming of day. . . . [And] it is not the least of its terrors that this evil thing is rooted deep in all good; in soil barren of holy memories it cannot rest."

Three-shot

HARKER
Doctor, please!

Van Helsing refers to the journal.

VAN HELSING
I take it we are all acquainted with the extraordinary facts in these most incredible journals?

Harker and Mina assent.

VAN HELSING
Strange and terrible as it is—it is true. I will pledge my life on it.
(*pauses, sits back from his dinner*)
So, Mr. Harker, now I must ask you, as your doctor, a sensitive question. During your "infidelity" with those creatures . . . those demonic women—
(*important*)
—did you, even for an instant—taste of their blood?

Van Helsing fixes his hypnotic gaze on Harker.

HARKER
(*shaking his head*)
No.

VAN HELSING
(*truly relieved*)
Good. Then you have not infected your blood with the terrible disease that destroyed poor Lucy.

Harker is a new man at the news.

HARKER
No . . . Doctor, you must understand—I doubted everything—even my mind. I was impotent with fear.

VAN HELSING
Ah, so!

HARKER
(*grim*)
But, sir—I know where the bastard sleeps. I brought him there—to Carfax Abbey.

VAN HELSING
Vampires do exist. This one we fight, this one we face, has the strength of twenty people, and you can testify to that, Mr. Harker. He can command the meaner things: the bat . . . the rodent . . . the wolf . . . and all the elements. He can come in mist and vapor and fog, and vanish at will. He can do all these things, yet he, this Dracula . . .

Suddenly he throws an ancient coin on the table.

VAN HELSING
. . . can be killed.

Jonathan reacts at the name. Mina reaches out, taking his hand.

Superimpose: close shot—the coin
We see the image of Dracula on it.

[*Asylum—Carfax in view—evening*]
Wide low angle

Music in. The "Vampire Killers" assembled. Winds rise. Holmwood tends two hunting dogs, tugging and yowling. Quincey and Harker bear revolvers and rifles, knives in their belts, torches, axes. Seward stands with Van Helsing, who totes only his bag like a doctor making a call. Mina is there as well. The men are clearly protecting her.

VAN HELSING (O.S.)
. . . Then how can we destroy him? Because we have the help of God. With His help, we poison the boxes of native soil in which the vampire must rest. With the things of God: the wafer, the cross, the holy water. And then we burn, for though the devil lives in hell, in his earthly body he is afraid of fire. We must find the boxes of his native earth in which he hides. Search well, for if we fail, then he will surely win. And he wins more than lives. Souls, my friends. He wins souls to whom forever the gates of Heaven are shut. So search. Find. Destroy.

Two-shot—Mina and Harker
Harker gathers his axe and gear.

MINA
I almost feel pity for anything so hunted as is this Count—

View on asylum window
Renfield—his shadowy figure behind the barred window watches Mina and Harker in silence. He sniffs the air, scenting like an animal.

RENFIELD
(to the distant Mina)
I can smell him on you. . . .

Medium shot
Seward enters to escort Mina back to the asylum.

SEWARD
I'll take her to my quarters.

They head toward the asylum as Harker joins the Vampire Killers heading toward Carfax.

The Vampire Killers assemble. "My friends, we are going into terrible danger, and we need arms of many kinds."

Eiko Ishioka supervises a fitting of one of Lucy's costumes.

"It was clear from the beginning," says Francis Coppola, "that the script was envisaged for a group of very young actors. So I said, then let's spend our money not on the sets but on the costumes, because the costumes are the thing closest to the actors. Let's dress these young actors in beautiful, exotic, erotic costumes that have so much of the emotion right in the fabric."

To incarnate his visual ideas for *Dracula*, Coppola asked the celebrated Japanese designer Eiko Ishioka to design the costumes. Known worldwide for her innovative work in graphic design, Eiko had created the production design for Paul Shrader's *Mishima*, the stage play *M. Butterfly*, Philip Glass's opera *The Making of the Representative for Planet 8*, and Faerie Tale Theater's *Rip Van Winkle* for television, where she first worked with Coppola. "By bringing in Eiko," he explains, "I knew I was insuring that at least one element of the film would be completely atypical, absolutely new, and unique."

Because *Dracula* was shot in the studio using what Coppola originally envisioned as minimal sets, the costumes had to take center stage. They were intended to create an arresting effect; to establish characters, period, mood, and the overall atmosphere of the film—in other words, to function as "a set design worn by the characters."

"Costumes should be more than just items that explain the role of the actors who wear them," says Eiko. "Costumes must have enough force to

The finished version of Mina's red dress and Eiko's original sketch for the costume.

Sketch for Dracula's royal cloak.

challenge the actors, the cinematographer, scenic designer, and director. And at times, the costumes should challenge the audience and make them think about why the actor is wearing that costume."

Eiko's background, as a Japanese exposed to visual culture from all over the world, uniquely equipped her to interpret the mingling of East and West in the story. Some of the Victorian dresses, for example, were made with Japanese *obi* (sash) fabric. Like Coppola, she drew on a vast range of visual sources for inspiration, from Symbolist paintings to Buddhist figurines to the Australian frilled lizard (the source for Lucy's bizarre wedding dress). But "reference is only reference," she notes. "I never use a design element straight from the source."

The costumes use a symbolic language to denote character traits. Red, the color of blood and passion, is reserved for Dracula's costumes—except for the red dress worn by Mina when she dances with Dracula at Rule's Cafe. White, black, and gold are also important in Dracula's costuming. Mina's clothes are mainly green, reflecting her youth, simplicity, and naiveté. Lucy and Mina wear similar green dresses in a party

The richly gilded pattern of the cloak was based on Gustav Klimt's paintings.

scene, but the embroidery—Mina's of leaves and Lucy's of snakes—differs significantly.

Associate costume designer Richard Shissler was crucial in translating much of Eiko's conceptual work into reality. With Eiko's strong streak of perfectionism and her desire to create museum-quality work, many of the costumes were one-of-a-kind. "We probably should have had duplicates of everything, but we just didn't have the budget," says Shissler.

"Eiko didn't want to compromise, so we had multiples only when we really needed them."

Eiko sat in on several early reading sessions of the screenplay to develop a comprehensive visual image of the film. "I felt like a sculptor, carefully putting my chisel into a chunk of rough marble. There were countless possibilities—but when I heard the actors speak the lines, the direction I should take became clear to me."

On Van Helsing
We pan him to a two-shot with Quincey.

VAN HELSING
Mr. Morris—your bullets will not harm him—he must be dismembered. I suggest you use your big knife.

QUINCEY
I wasn't planning on gettin' that close, Doc.

Tracking with Mina and Seward
walking to the asylum. She turns to watch the men leaving.

On Renfield
hanging out his window as the men enter Carfax

RENFIELD
(shouts over and over)
Master! Master!

THE MAN WHO WOULD BE IMMORTAL

"'I am a sane man fighting for his soul' . . . a very great line," wrote Francis Coppola in his notes. "Renfield is not a vampire but he is an infected party, like Harker. So how do we portray him? . . . I want to cast Tom Waits and I don't mind if he knows it."

Tom Waits, who plays Dr. Seward's "zoöphagous" patient Renfield, has worked with Coppola on

music for *The Outsiders*, *Rumble Fish*, *The Cotton Club*, and the Oscar-nominated score for *One from the Heart*. The internationally known singer and actor began writing and performing in his native Los Angeles, living in a car and working as a nightclub doorman. He established a longtime performing residency as the Tropicana Hotel, a legendary haven for traveling musicians.

Waits' musical style is unmistakable but elusive; one writer called it "bohemian word-jazz mixed with the blues." His trade-mark whiskey-rasped voice was first heard on the 1973 album "Closing Time," and his 1975 double live album, "Nighthawks at the Diner," remains among his most popular recordings.

Waits first appeared on screen in 1979 in Sylvester Stallone's *Paradise Alley*, and he first won notice in Jim Jarmusch's *Down By Law*. He has also appeared in *Ironweed*, *Queen's*

Logic, and *At Play in the Fields of the Lord*, and starred in his own concert film *Big Time*. He has co-authored a play for Chicago's Steppenwolf Theater, as well as appearing in stage productions there and in Los Angeles. He composed the score and co-authored songs for Jarmusch's *Night on Earth*, and collaborated with director Robert Wilson and writer William Burroughs on an opera, *The Black Rider*, which premiered in 1990. Another collaboration with Wilson, *Alice in Wonderland*, will premiere in late 1992, and a new album was released earlier that year.

Waits was a legend to the mostly young cast of *Dracula*, who felt privileged to spend time on the set with him. "When he was reading Renfield, people would just laugh, he was so great," remembers Keanu Reeves. "One time at lunch, he sat down at the piano and sang 'Waltzing Matilda' for Winona."

[Asylum corridor—night]

Master—tracking shot
in front of Seward, escorting Mina down the corridor. They pass by Renfield, at his cell door. He seethes.

RENFIELD
Master—I am here!

Mina slows and turns, startled. Seward tries to hurry her along. She resists.

MINA
Dr. Seward, who is that man?

SEWARD
Mr. Renfield. This is no place for you, Madam Mina—

MINA
(instantly drawn)
Renfield? I must see him.

We track in more as she moves closer to the cell, Seward trying to keep her at a safe distance, moving into a medium three-shot.

SEWARD
Renfield, behave yourself, now. This is Mrs. Harker.

Closeup Renfield
Renfield properly bows, eyeing her through the bars; lucid, calm.

RENFIELD
Good evening.

Closeup Mina

MINA
Good evening, Mr. Renfield.

RENFIELD
It seems I've been rather naughty.

He looks her deep in the eye. His eyes grow fearful.

RENFIELD
I know you. You're the bride my Master covets!

MINA
I have a husband. I am Mrs. Harker.

Single on Seward
observing.

RENFIELD
My Master tells me about you.

Leonard Wolf, from *The Annotated Dracula*, on Renfield:

" 'The Master is at hand.' With this brusque announcement Renfield casts himself into the role of an anti-John-the-Baptist announcing the coming of the anti-Christ.

" 'The blood is the life!' Though Renfield is quick to quote Scripture here, his keepers might have reminded him that his doglike blood lapping is scripturally forbidden. 'The blood is the life' comes from Deuteronomy 12:23, but the whole verse reads, 'Only be sure that thou eat not the blood: for the blood is the life; and thou mayest not eat the life with the flesh.' Nor is this the only place in the Bible where blood-drinking is prohibited."

129

"I am a sane man fighting for his soul!"

RENFIELD
Master! Master! You promised me eternal life—but you give it to the pretty woman! Seward pulls Mina away, hurrying her down the corridor. We stay on Renfield.

RENFIELD
Dr. Jack! I am no lunatic! I'm a sane man fighting for his soul!

[Seward's quarters—night]

Wide shot
Seward bids Mina goodbye, kissing her hand as he leaves. We can still hear Renfield shouting offstage.

SEWARD
You'll be completely safe here.

We track closer with Mina to the window. We go over her shoulder to see Carfax out the window.

[Carfax chapel—night]

Wide low angle tracking
with the Vampire Killers, surveying the eerie sight, walking through the row of boxes. Light from the torches falls on the boxes. Harker inspects one, adrenalin rushing.

Low angle
Dracula as the bat, hanging. We move into his face.

VAN HELSING
The sacred earth of his homeland. Destroy every box. Sterilize the earth inside. Leave him no refuge. Let the exorcism begin.

On Harker
He takes the lead, fire axe in hand. He surges, driving the axe through the lid with a cry of rage. He chops again—moving to the next—smashing it—
Closeup on bat.

On Van Helsing
He removes a flask of holy water from his bag, hanging it about his neck.

On Holmwood and Quincey
dumping the white moldy earth—

Back to Van Helsing
He sprinkles the earth with holy water and plants lit candles and crucifixes in the defiled dirt, while reciting the exorcism ritual:

MINA
What does he tell you?

RENFIELD
That he is coming . . . he is coming for you.
(motions her closer)
Please don't stay here—get away from these men . . . please. I pray God I may never see your sweet face again.
(kisses her hand lying on the bars)
May God bless you and keep you.

Back to master
Mina is disturbed and fascinated by Renfield. Suddenly Renfield erupts, smashing his head against the bars.

VAN HELSING
(Latin)
I adjure you, ancient serpent, by the judge
of the living and the dead, by your Creator,
by the Creator of the whole universe, by
Him who has the power to consign you to
hell, to depart forthwith in fear.

High angle—pixilation POV
The men doing their dirty business. Hearts
pounding—blood glowing in their veins—
breathing amplified. We hear Dracula's
metallic growl.

Pixilation POV starts moving
Bat Dracula flies out of the chapel to the
asylum, in the direction of Renfield's window.

[Seward's quarters—night]

Mina in her bed gown sits on the bed. Renfield's painful cries continue offscreen. She
covers her ears—wanting him to stop. We
track with Mina to the window.

RENFIELD (V.O.)
You cannot have her. . . .

[Carfax—grounds]

Mina's POV—out the window
In the distance, the small flickering light of
the torches. A thin streak of absinthe-green
mist snakes across the grass toward the asylum, almost invisible.

RENFIELD (V.O.)
I tried to warn her. She would not listen to
me. She will be spared, Master. You cannot
have her—

[Renfield's cell—continuing action]

Pan down the wall
with the green mist to reveal Renfield in the
corner, in high wide angle.

DRACULA (O.S.)
Renfield . . . you betrayed me.

Renfield looks up in shock.

RENFIELD
No, master! No, I serve only you. . . I serve
only you!

We see Renfield apparently hurling himself
head first repeatedly against the bars—a
lunatic purging his personal demons.

[Asylum—Renfield's cell]

Wide low angle
Renfield is embedded in the bars, dying, a
twisted mass. A keeper runs in.

[Chapel—night]

Wide shot
Harker chops. The others stack the boxes
high. Seward arrives, running to join the
others. Quincey methodically spreads coal
oil on the pile—high-pitched squealing
echoes from below.

Low angle shot—on the floor
We see rats coming out from under the
boxes, from a swirl of sparkling mist rushing

*The hunters destroy
Dracula's boxes at
Carfax and purify the
soil.*

131

across the floor—we track in front of the rats running towards camera. They climb on Harker; the others pull them off.

VAN HELSING
Call the dogs!

Wider shot
Harker tosses his torch onto the pile of boxes. It erupts in a ball of flames—

[Seward's quarters—bedroom—night]

Slow pan from the door
(Music cue.) Following the green mist as it enters through window, down wall, to the end of the bed. Then up the bed, following the bulge under Mina's sheets, coiling toward her like a serpent (reverse action)—ending on a closeup of Mina, asleep.

MINA
(in her sleep)
Oh, my love—yes—you found me—

132

Above: *A deadly mist emerges from Carfax Abbey.* Opposite: *Sätty art of swarming rats from* The Annotated Dracula.

DRACULA
Mina . . . my most precious life—

MINA
(in her sleep)
I have wanted this to happen. I know that now. I want to be with you—always—

Mina's POV—Dracula
sliding from underneath the sheet in front of her face, handsome—looking at her passionately. We pull back into a two-shot.

DRACULA
You cannot know what you are saying.

Closeup Mina
Her eyes open.

MINA
Yes . . . I do know.

She kisses him, heat building. She opens her legs and buries his face in her neck—

Visual effects supervisor Roman Coppola:

"When we were creating the green mist, we experimented with a sort of puppet, a cloudlike marionette that was maneuvered by someone on one side of a 50/50 mirror. As in all those old mirror effects, bringing the light source up or down controls how the image appears, and the lighting could make it green. But, as was pointed out to me, the puppet didn't look like mist, no matter what we used. So we ended up using dry ice smoke, lit green and superimposed on the set with a 50/50 mirror. The final cut includes some optical FX as well."

Dracula finds his princess.

MINA
But you live! You live! What are you? I must know. You must tell me.

DRACULA
I am nothing. Lifeless, soulless—hated—feared. I am dead to all the world. Hear me: I am the monster the breathing men would kill! I am Dracula.

Mina breaks down, all her faculties collapsing, pounding him futilely—her own guilt fueling her. Dracula turns away, covering his face in shame as she flails him, weeping. We superimpose image of old Dracula (projected on his face).

MINA
(confessing)
I love you. . . . God forgive me . . . I do!

His entire being swells with the power—the hunger. He turns slowly to face her—his face once again young, beautiful—filled with eternal tender love for this incredible woman.

Extreme closeup Dracula over Mina
Dracula rises above her, holding her gently in his hands, as in a vampire wedding.

MINA
I want to be what you are. See what you see—love what you love.

DRACULA
Mina—to walk with me you must die to your breathing life and be reborn to mine.

MINA
You are my love—and my life. Always—

He enfolds her, bends her backward gently.

DRACULA
Then—I give you life eternal. Everlasting love. The power of the storm. And the beasts of the earth. Walk with me—to be my loving wife . . . forever.

MINA
Yes—I will—yes—

Wider shot
Dracula caresses her face as tenderly as a child. She is willing. She is ready. He gently turns her, exposing her neck, kissing her softly.

sliding him down to her breasts. Her gown slips down her pale shoulders—his mouth meets her flesh. Her legs wrap around his waist. She arches against him.

MINA
I was so afraid I would never feel your touch again—I feared you were dead.

Dracula stops at her throat—her pulse pounding in his brain. He grabs her hand, placing her palm over his bare chest—over his heart. She stiffens—the realization—

Closeup Dracula

DRACULA
There is no life in this body . . .

Two-shot
She shrinks back in revulsion—horrified.

DRACULA
I take you as my eternal bride—

She moans in ecstasy—a tiny grimace of
pain as he enters her veins.

Closeup—his chest
With his long thumbnail, he opens a vein
over his heart. We see his beating heart.

DRACULA
—flesh of my flesh—blood of my blood. . . .
Mina. . . . Drink and join me in eternal
life—

He pulls her submissively to his chest. She
drinks. She swoons as his life runs into her.

Reverse angle on Dracula
He falters—tears welling up—suddenly
fighting his desire. He shoves her back in
anguish.

DRACULA
I cannot let this be!

MINA
Please—I don't care—make me yours.

DRACULA
You will be cursed—as I am—to walk in the
shadow of death for all eternity. I love you
too much—to condemn you!

She shudders—pleading, holding him,
caressing him.

MINA
Take me away from all this death!

She forces her lips back to his chest. His
moans of ecstasy build to a climax; then he
wraps her in his arms, holds her close.

Wide shot on door
The door bursts open and we pull back to
see Van Helsing and the men at the doorway. They freeze—seeing only Mina, her
head posed as if drinking from Dracula's
breast.

*The vampire wedding
sacrament.*

135

THE HORROR OF SEX

"Vampires seduce us and take us to dark places and awaken us sexually in ways that are taboo," observes screenwriter James Hart. "The vampire comes and says, 'I'm going to kill you and you're going to love it—and not only that, you're going to want more.'"

A fearful fascination with sex is a hallmark of Victorian fiction, nowhere more so than in Bram Stoker's *Dracula*. His vampires represent, among other things, the rampant libido, "sex reeking of the full perfume of the swamp," as Leonard Wolf says. Stoker's human characters, even the straightlaced Jonathan Harker, are irresistibly drawn to them—but if they surrender, they are doomed. Only death and a holy ritual of exorcism can save their souls.

Women, at least in fiction, have been particularly vulnerable to the vampire's erotic appeal, and their punishment has reflected women's sexual repression throughout history. In *Dracula*, "Lucy represents the burgeoning, youthful woman who was desperately trying to fulfill herself and her desires," Hart says. "None of the men around her are capable of doing that for her. Only Dracula satisfies her—but, of course, destroys her."

The women in *Dracula* live out the men's sexual fantasies, it has been pointed out, and pay the price. As George Stade has written, "The prevailing emotion of the novel is a screaming horror of female sexuality." In his feverish curiosity and shame about sex, Stoker typified his times.

Philip Burne-Jones's painting The Vampire *scandalized London when it appeared in 1897, the year* Dracula *was published. The model was English actress Mrs. Patrick Campbell.*

HARKER
Mina!—

Medium closeup—Bat Dracula
comes from nowhere, swooping down, his eyes red with rage. Mina, in the background, wails in guilt and horror. We pull back as Dracula springs at them—catlike—protecting her.

On men over Dracula (Mina's POV)
Seward and Holmwood with guns drawn.

Closeup Van Helsing
Van Helsing advances, raising a large crucifix. As Dracula approaches, the shot becomes an over shoulder Dracula on Van Helsing. Power against power. Van Helsing and Dracula face to face.

Medium shot
on Bat Dracula over Van Helsing.

DRACULA
Old fool—You think you can destroy me with your idols—

He snarls horribly and the crucifix in front of his face bursts into flames.

DRACULA (CONTINUES)
I, who served the cross—I, who commanded nations hundreds of years before you were born!

VAN HELSING
(shouting over a raging wind)
Your armies were defeated. You murdered thousands with unspeakable tortures.

DRACULA
I was betrayed! Look what your God has done to me.

VAN HELSING
Your war against God is over—now you must pay for your crimes.

He dashes holy water into Dracula's face. It burns him like acid; he wails in pain. Harker runs to Mina, shielding her.

DRACULA
My revenge has just begun. And she, your best beloved, is now my flesh, my blood, my kin—my bride!

Medium shot
favoring Harker.

HARKER
No!

Harker puts himself in front of Mina and fires his revolver pointblank at Dracula.

Close shot
Dracula bleeds.

Closeup Van Helsing

VAN HELSING
Leave her to God!

It burns his skin like acid—he wails in pain. Taking a final longing look at Mina, Dracula bows and backs away into the dark shadows of the room. We see only his red eyes.

Go to black

VAN HELSING
More light! Get me more light!

A lamp is lifted, revealing a figure made of rats in the shape of Dracula. It crumbles into individual rats scurrying away, all over

the men, and then escaping from the room out the window

On window
The men rush to the window peering out.

Their POV—out window
Carfax burning. Dracula is gone. Silence.

Medium shot
Move in on Mina, covering herself. Blood on her face.

MINA
(breaking down)
Unclean—unclean—

Superimpose:
[Carfax—night]

Tracking shot
along the burning boxes, earth, smoke. (Music in.) The camera slowly tracks through the burning debris and finds the photoplate of Mina—in flames.

"Look what your God has done to me!"

THE MANY FACES OF DRACULA

One of Dracula's chief qualities as a vampire is his ability to transform himself into many shapes and aspects—a challenge for the makeup artists who mold faces and bodies for the camera, and for the actors who must inhabit them.

At one count, Gary Oldman had ten manifestations of his character. There was Dracula as the 15th-century prince, his visage based on old woodcut illustrations; as the Dark Driver of the caleche; as the 400-year-old nobleman with hair lining his palms; as a demonic beast that is half man and half wolf, and later as a true wolf. "Part of the vampire myth is that they turn into wolves," says Francis Coppola, "and have power over wolves and low creatures."

"Vampires also have an affiliation with the bat, and so you also see Dracula as a bat creature," in the climactic scene where he confronts Van Helsing and the other Vampire Killers over Mina. Earlier he appears as a dashing young Victorian

The wolfen Dracula with Lucy.

dandy on the streets of London, and on two occasions with a ravaged death face. Three other incarnations—as an elusive green mist, a molting chrysalis, and a startling assemblage of rats on a human frame—owe their existence to the special effects team.

All of the looks portrayed by Gary Oldman were created by special effect makeup artist Greg Cannom, with his associate Matthew Mungle, and wig and hair overseer Stuart Artingstall. Cannom spent several months conceiving the designs with Coppola and costume designer Eiko Ishioka before shooting began. "The great thing about Francis," Cannom says, "is that he would get so excited in our early meetings—he painted such vivid pictures in my mind, it was easy to

come up with the designs for the film."

Cannom's most difficult job was the old-age makeup, the first of many looks he designed for the film. After experimenting with Maggie Smith's 90-year-old woman in *Hook*, he perfected a translucent appearance where, even through all the layers, individual veins can be seen. Every application of the old-age Dracula makeup took four hours, with 12 foam latex appliances on Oldman's face and five on each hand. A further ordeal was posed by hard scleral contact lenses that turned his eyes red but could be worn for no more than 30 minutes at a time.

At one point Oldman suffered a severe allergic reaction to one of the chemicals used to set the prosthetic makeup, and a double briefly replaced him in the wolf-beast suit. Even under the makeup, however, viewers on the set could sense the difference.

"The great challenge of all that stuff," says Oldman, whose favorite wardrobe is jeans and a t-shirt, "is that you mustn't let prosthetic makeup or costumes wear you. You have to wear them, and have the energy to make the performance and the character come through all this plastic."

Left: *The bat Dracula.* Above: *Latex molds for several of Dracula's monstrous faces.*

VAN HELSING (V.O.)

He has escaped us for the time being. We found and destroyed all his places of refuge—all but one. Our work is not over; there is but one more earth-box in which he hides as he is carried back to his native soil. We must try to find it; when that is done all may yet be well. We have learnt something—much! Notwithstanding his brave words, he fears us; he fears time, he fears want! For if not, why does he hurry so?

VAN HELSING (V.O.)

Where is he now, Mina? Where is your dark prince?

MINA (V.O.)

He is gone. . . .

VAN HELSING (V.O.)

How do you know, child?

MINA (V.O.)

He . . . speaks to me.

VAN HELSING (V.O.)

Mina, in whose veins his blood flows, and who feels the flow of his mind, can help us. We will take her with us right into the heart of the enemy's country, and in her mind, by means of hypnosis, we will come upon the enemy's trail.

Dissolve to:

[Seward's quarters—night]

Low angle closeup
Van Helsing comes into frame, holding a lit candle. He is worn, aged with the stress and rigor. He looks at Mina.

Closeup Mina
She stares into space. Gaunt. Pale. Her gums receding back. She is changing. Transforming. We pull back to reveal Van Helsing sitting by her bed.

VAN HELSING

He has a strong mind connection to you. His heart was strong enough to survive the grave.

MINA

You . . . admire him.

Closeup Van Helsing over Mina

VAN HELSING

Ja. He was in life a most remarkable man. His mind is great and powerful, but greater is the necessity to stamp him out and destroy him utterly.

Reverse on Mina over Van Helsing
She nods with firm conviction.

MINA

Doctor—I know I am becoming like him. When I find in myself a sign of harm to anyone I love, I shall die.

VAN HELSING

You must not die—your salvation is his destruction. That is why I want to hypnotize you, Mina. Help me find him—before it is too late. Help me, Mina.

Storyboard art, a Dracula made of rats. To film this shot, "rats" were glued to an armature, and the shot of them scattering was done as a match cut.

Here Jonathan interrupted him harshly: "Do you mean to say, Professor Van Helsing, that you would bring Mina, in her sad case and tainted as she is with that devil's illness, right into the jaws of his death-trap? Not for the world!. . .

"Remember," [replied Van Helsing] "that we are in terrible straits. If the Count escape us this time—and he is strong and subtle and cunning—he may choose to sleep for a century; and then in time our dear one"—he took my hand—"would come to him to keep him company, and would be as those others that you, Jonathan, saw. You have told us of their gloating lips; you heard their ribald laugh. . . . You shudder; and well may it be. Forgive me that I make you so much pain, but it is necessary."

Van Helsing hypnotically caresses her hand, moving the candle slowly before her—mesmerizing her. She fixes on it—weak, fatigued—

Superimpose:
Ghost image of Dracula putting his hands on her shoulders, caressing her; then it fades. We track in on Mina's eyes.

VAN HELSING
Look at this flame, this light. . . . Light of all lights. . . . I want you to sleep. Sleep now.

MINA
(drifting)
Yes. I must go to him. He calls.

VAN HELSING (O.S.)
What do you hear, child?

We hear these sounds: Lapping waves, rushing water, and creaking masts.

Insert—stormy sea

MINA (O.S.)
Mother ocean . . .

VAN HELSING (O.S.)
What do you see?

Dissolve to:
[The ship Czarina Catherine—*the hold]*

Tracking shot (Mina's face superimposed)
Left to right over cargo, to one box resting in the shadows.

[Seward's quarters]

Double exposure—Dracula's face

VAN HELSING (V.O.)
Where are you going?

[Train—day]
Tracing its way along the edge of Mina's face, superimposed.

MINA (V.O.)
I am drifting, floating . . . home, home. Sleep has no place it can call its own—I hear men's voices talking in strange tongues. . . . fierce, falling water and howling of wolves. I am still. . . so still. . . and it is like death.

Dissolve to:
[Private railroad car—day]

Close on Mina
Deep in hypnotic trance. Calm, serene smile.

MINA
Home . . . Home . . .
We pull back to see Van Helsing enter frame and gently lift Mina's lip to reveal her growing fangs. She sleeps.

Two-shot—Van Helsing and Seward
Seward unpacks transfusion tubes. Van Helsing stops him.

VAN HELSING
The vampire has baptized her with his own blood. Her blood is dying, my friend.

Two-shot—Harker and Mina
Mina suddenly grabs Harker, barely able to breathe. Harker holds her, fighting his tears.

HARKER
Mina—I will not let you go into the unknown alone.

Back to Van Helsing and Seward
Van Helsing motions to Seward; they exit,

leaving Harker and Mina alone. We slowly track in on them.

MINA
My poor dear Jonathan, what have I done to you?

HARKER
No . . . no . . . no . . . I have done this to both of us.

MINA
I can hear the waves lapping against his ship. The wind is high; he calls me to him.

Mina wrestles with the powers ripping her insides—Harker can no longer hold back his tears. Mina smiles lovingly, raising her hand to wipe his tears. Tracking shot ends on closeup Mina. Her hand falls back. She is weaker.

MINA
I'm so cold . . . so . . . cold.

Van Helsing hypnotizes Mina.

Act IV

Love Never Dies

[*Private railroad car—night*]

Superimpose:
Harker's journal

HARKER (V.O.)
"28 October. We have beaten the *Czarina Catherine*, with her devil's cargo, to the Roumanian port of Varna. We are well supplied with money and horses, courtesy of Quincey and Holmwood."

Close shot—a map
Train schedules, a pocket watch, rail schedule.

HARKER (V.O.)
"Mina is worse every day. She is in his mind, and leads us to him. Arrangement has been made with certain officials that the instant the Count is seen, we are to be informed by a special messenger. Fortunately this is a country where bribery can do anything.

View on Mina
sleeping. Van Helsing at her side.

HARKER (V.O.)
"I no longer fear this monster. I will be the first to board his ship and find his box. God keep me strong, for mine must be the arm that strikes the first blow."

Right: *Production drawing of a railroad siding in Transylvania, staging point for the Vampire Killers.* Opposite: *They plan their strategy.*

Wide shot
Holmwood in his bush gear and fur parka hurries in with a cablegram—distraught.

HARKER (V.O.)
"Noon. Holmwood received a wire from his clerk at Lloyds. The Count's ship sailed past us in the night fog to the northern port at Galatz. He knew we were waiting for him."

We push in on Van Helsing and Holmwood as Van Helsing reads the telegram.

Harker, Seward, and Quincey
The men look at each other in shock.

VAN HELSING
The black devil is reading Mina's mind. He knows every move we make.

Wide shot
Harker springs into action, taking up the map on the table. He indicates Dracula's position and theirs.

Dr. Seward's Diary

"Jonathan," she said, and the word sounded like music on her lips it was so full of love and tenderness. "Jonathan dear, and you all my true, true friends, I want you to bear something in mind through all this dreadful time. I know that you must fight—that you must destroy even as you destroyed the false Lucy so that the true Lucy might live hereafter; but it is not a work of hate. That poor soul who has wrought all this misery is the saddest case of all. Just think what will be his joy when he too is destroyed in his worser part that his better part may have spiritual immortality. You must be pitiful to him too, though it may not hold your hands from his destruction."

Dr. Seward's Diary

Here Quincey Morris added: "I understand that the Count comes from a wolf country and it may be that he shall get there before us. I propose that we add Winchesters to our armament. I have a kind of belief in a Winchester when there is any trouble of that sort around. Do you remember, Art, when we had the pack after us at Tobolsk? What wouldn't we have given then for a repeater apiece?"

Mina Harker's Journal

Professor Van Helsing and I are to leave by the 11.40 train to-night for Veresti, where we are to get a carriage to drive to the Borgo Pass. We are bringing a good deal of ready money, as we are to buy a carriage and horses. We shall drive ourselves, as we have no one whom we can trust in the matter. The Professor knows something of a great many languages, so we shall get on all right. We have all got arms, even for me. . . . Dear Dr. Van Helsing comforts me by telling me that I am fully armed as there may be wolves; the weather is getting colder every hour, and there are snow-flurries which come and go as warnings.

Above: *Van Helsing and Mina make their way toward Castle Dracula.* Opposite: *The castle in the distance, production drawing.*

Dissolve to:
[Railroad siding—day]

Matte shot
The men unload horses from a railroad boxcar.

VAN HELSING (V.O.)
From Galatz it is several days' journey to the castle. The others will head north on horseback and try to cut him off in the mountain passes.

Grim silence. Holmwood enters frame. The men clasp each other in their solemn oath.

VAN HELSING (CONTINUED)
He must not reach his castle—the closer he gets, the stronger he becomes. I will go with Mina directly to the castle—it is only a few days' ride from here. If the others fail, Madam Mina and I will be waiting for him.

Close on the men's hands
They pull apart to reveal Mina coming to them. There is a gleam of triumph in her vacant smile. We pull back as Quincey hands Mina a sealskin rifle scabbard holding a well-oiled Winchester.

Insert—Castle Dracula exterior

Dissolve to:
[Borgo Road—day]

Wide high angle
Great winds. We see Dracula's beloved snowcapped peaks on one side, the abyss on the other. Mina and Van Helsing's coach,

small on the bottom of the frame, moves towards us. *(Note: from this point on there will be increasing cold.)*

Over two horses
We slowly move in on Van Helsing and Mina in their coach; both wearing bulky fur. The horses are fatigued. The old man even more so. Mina reclines in a near comatose state. Suddenly, she wakes, animated, excited as a child—

Mina's POV—moving shot
They round a sharp turn. The castle appears in full view on its crag of rock. A timeless sentinel. The road shrinc of the wolfen anti-Christ marks the spot.

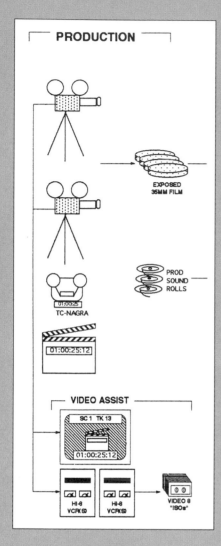

PRODUCTION

EXPOSED 35MM FILM

TC-NAGRA

01:00:25:12

PROD SOUND ROLLS

VIDEO ASSIST

SC 1 TK 13

01:00:25:12

HI-8 VCR(S)

HI-8 VCR(S)

VIDEO 8 "ISOs"

*D*racula has the distinction of being the first major motion picture to go through editing and post-production entirely in the electronic domain—that is, to be cut and sound-edited on videotape with the aid of computers. This was made possible by a history of experimentation in film technology at Francis Coppola's production company, American Zoetrope.

"Francis is a gadgeteer," explains Kim Aubry, Zoetrope vice president for engineering and new technology, with a smile. "He has put a lot of effort and money into developing hardware and software to advance film technology.

"Francis's idea is that the stages of pre-production, production, and post-production should not be isolated, separate steps, but rather simultaneous and integrated."

Individual technologies pioneered by TV, commercial production, and music videos had been applied to some stages of filmmaking—editing, scoring, sound mixing—but "no one had put all the black boxes together to effectively post-produce a major film in a short time," says Aubry. What the Zoetrope team did on *Dracula* was the equivalent of hooking up a network of word processors, bringing the information-management advantages of computers to film.

Coppola has been a firm believer in "electronic cinema," a term he coined, since his 1981 production *One from the Heart.* During the 1980s, Zoetrope's low-budget unit, Commercial Pictures (headed by Roman Coppola) used the computer-controlled Montage editing system on several of their projects. The Montage was later used successfully on parts of *Godfather III.* Encouraged by the comprehensive notes his technical team had made during the process, Coppola decided that *Dracula* would be his first feature cut electronically from beginning to end.

The Montage system permits nonlinear, random-access picture editing, which greatly streamlines the process of tracking and accessing frames of film. Says Aubry, "Data about every frame of exposed film and production sound recorded on the set lives in a database in a couple of laptop computers, along with a brief description of the scene. We know its scene take number, its date of production, its camera roll, sound roll, negative key number, videotape time-code transfer number, and production audio time-code number."

With a smaller version of the editing system housed in his production trailer (known as the Silverfish and also equipped with espresso machine), Coppola can begin working with footage as soon as it is shot. A video tap through the film camera feeds the image directly into his system. Editing is thus going on throughout the shoot, and by the end of principal photography, Coppola has something close to a "director's cut."

Aubry credits the cooperation of cinematographer Michael Ballhaus for making the process easier.

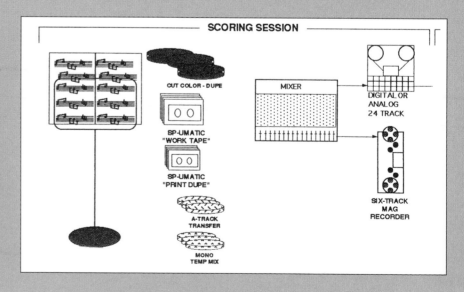

SCORING SESSION

CUT COLOR - DUPE

SP-UMATIC "WORK TAPE"

SP-UMATIC "PRINT DUPE"

A-TRACK TRANSFER

MONO TEMP MIX

MIXER

DIGITAL OR ANALOG 24 TRACK

SIX-TRACK MAG RECORDER

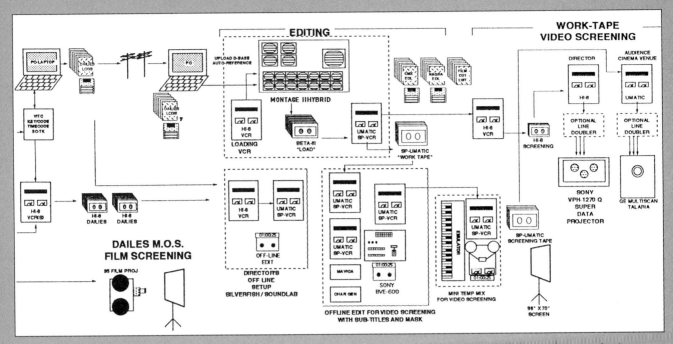

Portions of a yard-long flow chart created by Zoetrope's Kim Aubry, graphically depicting the electronic production and post-production process from principal photography through final 35mm answer print with Dolby™ sound.

"Michael agreed to allow us to provide him with mostly video dailies, and only a small amount of daily footage was workprinted—that reduced the initial lab costs quite a bit. He used the new Arriflex 535 camera, which puts time code on the film and makes it possible to synch up dailies electronically very fast."

The time-coding is also a key factor in electronic post-production, helping editors to easily synchronize film and sound without sacrificing quality. The challenge is "how to capture data on the set and then transmit it to the lab, picture editors, and sound editors," says Aubry, "while keeping the flexibility of the old manual logging system that's been used for 75 years."

Coppola's experiments have many commercial applications. Zoetrope collaborators have written new software that enables film-trained editors to manage the new computerized logs. They are also working with sound manufacturers to develop a completely computer-based sound editing and mixing system for large feature films.

New technology also helped the director stay in touch with his second unit on *Dracula*. Coppola says, "I always had two screens, so I could see the shots Roman was getting and talk to him any time, while he was three blocks away on another sound stage. That's the way it's going to be in the future—images piped around studios like hot and cold running water."

As with any new technology there are risks, Kim Aubry notes. Until recently this kind of experimentation has tended not to happen in Hollywood, where the stakes are high and the prestige of high-profile film artists is on the line. With Coppola's encouragement, however, the Zoetrope pioneers are taking the plunge, and lending encouragement to other film professionals who want to enter the brave new world of electronic moviemaking.

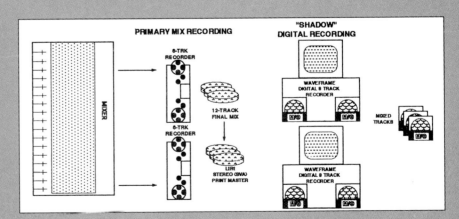

[Coach—continuing action]

Moving two-shot
Wind grow stronger. (Music cue.)

MINA
I know this place—

Adrenalin-charged, she fixes on the road shrine.

VAN HELSING
The end of the world . . .

MINA
We must go on.

Van Helsing studies Mina's exuberant reaction, troubled.

VAN HELSING
It is late, child. We rest here.

MINA
No—I must go! Please let me go—I must see him! He needs me—

She struggles to get out. He gently restrains her, taking her hand. The winds rise around them. Van Helsing listens, sensing a presence. The faint tingling of laughter echoes. He reluctantly drives on.

One-eighty-degree wide shot
The coach moving towards the castle.

[Borgo Road—day]

The hunters on the trail.

HARKER (V.O.)
"We have now passed beyond Bistritza. At Veresti, we learned that Dracula's gypsies took charge of the vampire's box and are on the Borgo Pass road. We are more than a day's ride from the castle, hours behind the Count. The dead travel fast, so we must ride through the night."

Superimpose:
map of the region

[Gypsy wagon—traveling—day]

Medium close head-on—four horses
Their heads racing toward camera, camera
moving in front of them. Camera booms up
to reveal a wagon with two Szgany gypsy
drivers. Camera booms up more to reveal a
single box strapped to the wagon, with five
mounted gypsies following on horseback.
Camera moves slowly in on the box.

[Dracula's box—day]

Dracula packed in the earth
We see part of his body exposed; we move
in on his face, half-submerged in the shifting earth. His handsome face has aged
again, rapidly.

DRACULA (V.O.)
Mina . . . you are near.

Dissolve to:
[Castle—promontory—night]

Master—close on the fire
(Music: percussion, winds.) We see Van
Helsing through the flames, as he throws
more wood on the roaring fire. We pan
with him to a wide two-shot with Mina.
Mina sits on her haunches on a couch of
furs, wide awake and energized by the night.
Van Helsing brings her a bowl of food.

VAN HELSING
You must eat something, child.

*Mina's vampire blood
grows stronger. Cop-
pola says, "Toward the
end of the movie, when
Mina starts to get sexy,
she should top Lucy."*

151

Above and opposite: *Mina tantalizes and then attacks Van Helsing.*

Memorandum by Abraham Van Helsing

It was as though all my memories of Jonathan's horrid experience were befooling me; for the snow flakes and the mist began to wheel and circle round, till I could get as though a shadowy glimpse of those women . . . the wheeling figures of mist and snow came closer, but keeping ever without the Holy circle. Then they began to materialise, till—if God have not taken away my reason, for I saw it through my eyes—there were before me in actual flesh the same three women that Jonathan saw in the room. . . I knew the round, swaying forms, the bright hard eyes, the white teeth, the ruddy color, the voluptuous lips. They smiled ever at poor dear Madam Mina; and as their laugh came through the silence of the night, they twined their arms and pointed at her, and said in those so sweet tingling tones: . . . "Come, sister. Come to us. Come! Come!"

MINA
(knocking the dish away)
I am not hungry!

We track sideways to see flames in the foreground and move in through the flames to Mina. Her eyes gleam. Van Helsing watches her. She begins to sway, transfixed, as we move in closer and closer on her. She chants the mother tongue, whispering guttural, strange words.

Closeup Van Helsing
He chills at the sight.

Closeup Mina
We hear the tingling laughter of the Brides offstage. Their faces appear briefly superimposed during the following scene. Horses whinny in fright. Mina responds, excited, possessed. She laughs giddily, bouncing on her haunches, wolfen, savage. She looks at Van Helsing. Her fur robe has come open, exposing her nipple; she brazenly leaves it open. She moves slowly toward Van Helsing, shameless, uninhibited.

MINA
You are so good to me, Professor. I know that Lucy harbored secret desires for you. She told me. I too know what men desire.

Back to Van Helsing
Aroused, weakening as she comes closer, into close two-shot. We pan with him as he bends . . . kissing her nipple. Her eyes glowing, she presses his mouth harder to her breast, waking his desires. When he's lost in her flesh, arching against her, Mina's eyes suddenly glow red.

MINA
Will you cut off my head and drive a stake through me as you did poor Lucy, you murdering bastard!

She jerks his head back in her powerful grip, exposing his neck. She opens her mouth, revealing newborn fangs erect in titillation. Van Helsing goes white, struggling away—

We hear offstage laughter of the Brides.

YOUNGEST BRIDE (O.S.)
(Roumanian)
Sister . . . take him first. Leave some sweets for us, sister. . . .

152

Right: *Van Helsing tries to calm Mina.* Opposite: *He drives off the Brides.*

THE VISIONARY DOCTOR VAN HELSING

The makers of *Dracula* were fortunate in securing British star Anthony Hopkins, fresh from his Oscar-winning performance in *The Silence of the Lambs*, to play Dr. Abraham Van Helsing. "I just wanted to work with Francis," Hopkins admits. "I said yes before I had read the script."

Bram Stoker created Van Helsing as Dracula's nemesis and antithesis. Coppola pushed Hopkins to shape the character in a more powerful way than he usually appears.

"On the other side of Dracula is Van Helsing, who's also somewhat demonic," the director notes. "I wanted Tony Hopkins, who has this wonderful madness of his own, to play him with a little orneriness and madness rather than as the kindly Dutch doctor—to make the Stoker character come alive more."

Hopkins was born in Wales and set his sights on acting at age 17. After local training and a stint in the military, he was accepted at the Royal Academy of Dramatic Art.

A few years of provincial repertory followed, and then he was invited to audition for Sir Laurence Olivier and the National Theatre at the Old Vic, where he performed many classic roles.

Hopkins made his film debut as Richard the Lionheart in Peter O'Toole's *The Lion in Winter*, and has since divided his time between theater, movies, and television in England and the U.S. Starring roles have included the TV miniseries *QB VII*, Captain Bligh in the film remake of *The Bounty*, and the Broadway production of *Equus*. He has appeared onstage in London in *M. Butterfly* and Shakespearean repertory. Other films include *The Elephant Man*, *A Bridge Too Far*, and most recently the Merchant-Ivory production of *Howard's End*. His television work has garnered two Emmys for Best Actor, and he was awarded the Commander of the Order of the British Empire by Queen Elizabeth in 1987.

Of Van Helsing, the actor says, "I think he's been down into the depths. He's done everything and seen the face of terror and death, and then comes out on the other side; he knows the nature of evil." He adds wryly, "I'm aware of another side of myself which I can draw on. I've played a few strange creatures."

VAN HELSING
Not while I live! I am vowed to protect you!

Closeup Van Helsing
Van Helsing tries to pull Mina off—she's fixed fast to him. He pulls a tin from his coat with his free hand and produces a holy wafer.

On Mina over Van Helsing
Van Helsing enters frame and presses the wafer to her forehead. Her skin sears at the touch. Mina screams, falling back, fangs disappearing. A scarlet red mark is branded on her forehead.

MINA
I am his—!

She convulses in gasping sobs, prostrate on the cold ground. Van Helsing kneels beside her, his tired body giving out. He grabs a stick from the fire and quickly draws a crude ring of flame around himself and Mina. He sprinkles holy water.

VAN HELSING
I have lost Lucy. I will not lose you to him. You are safe inside the ring!

MINA
Why fear for me? None is safer in all the world from them than me. I am their kind.

Camera pulls back and we see the two of them on the ground inside the circle.

YOUNGEST BRIDE (O.S.)
(Roumanian)
She is our sister!

Van Helsing waves the flaming stick.

Closeup Van Helsing

VAN HELSING
Satan's whores! Leave us! This is holy ground!

They draw nearer, taunting him. Then we see their leaping shadows and those of the horses, as the Brides slaughter and feed on them.

"Oh . . . but it was butcher work; had I not been nerved by thoughts of other dead, and of the living over whom hung such a pall of fear, I could not have gone on."

Van Helsing's cries fade, as the ring of fire dissolves into the morning sun, filling the frame.

[Castle promontory—sunrise]

Castle doors
Van Helsing emerges exhausted, his big fur coat matted and drenched in blood. His eyes deepset, profoundly changed. He slowly raises three freshly decapitated heads of the Brides!

On Van Helsing
He hurls the heads. His scream primal, triumphant.

The heads falling (matte shot)
into the Arges river far below.

Insert—Castle exterior

[Borgo Road—sunset]

Dracula's box
Dracula hears Van Helsing's cries of triumph.

Closeup on horses'
of the gypsy wagon carrying Dracula's box. Moves into closeup of horses' hooves.

[Castle promontory—sunset]

Medium closeup Mina
She stands on a rock formation, looking out into the distance. Van Helsing appears in the background. He staggers up to Mina, barely able to stand.

MINA
He comes!

VAN HELSING
They race the sunset. We may be too late— God help us.

Mina is agitated, her breathing labored. Wolves begin to howl offscreen. Van Helsing peers through his field glasses.

[Borgo Road—sunset]

Wide shot
The gypsy caravan heading toward camera. In the background four riders appear, closing fast—Quincey, giving his unforgettable rebel yell, flanked by Jack Seward, his saber drawn! Holmwood and Harker following. *(Note: all shots in this battle sequence are moving shots as wagon and horses approach the castle.)*

[Castle promontory—sunset]

Van Helsing and Mina
watching the action below.

VAN HELSING
Look, Madam Mina! Two horsemen follow fast! Hah! It must be Quincey and Jack!

He hands her the glasses. She looks.

[Borgo Road—sunset]

Wide shot
Horsemen following the wagon.

Close on Quincey
He fires his rifle rapidly, Indian style.

Close shot
A Szgany drops.

Mina and Van Helsing watch from the castle promontory as the chase draws near.

STAGING THE CHASE ON A SOUND STAGE

One of the most challenging sequences to film was the scene where the Vampire Killers pursue Dracula back to his castle on horseback through the Transylvanian Mountains.

The Borgo Pass set occupied all of Stage 15, the size of a football field and the largest in Hollywoood. The chase had to be managed on a more-or-less oval track built around the perimeter. Illuminated by lightning, pelted by falling "snow," and pushed by blowing wind, actors, horses, and wagons tore around the track as fast as they could. The grueling sequence was gaffed by stunt coordinator Billy Burton, using over 35 horses and 16 stuntmen.

Production designer Tom Sanders elaborates. "We put rock at one end of the stage to elevate the road, so it looks like it's going through the mountains, and the other end we kept on ground level with lots of trees, more like the countryside. By the way they shoot and cut it, it can look like hundreds of different miles of road, because the greensmen kept moving trees around to create different backgrounds.

"As they approach the castle, you see huge slabs and piles of quarried rock lying around. The idea was that Dracula has quarried out the surrounding mountains, has destroyed the land as well as the people around him. You'll see this in the wide shots of the castle model. And the river is ruined from sewage.

"The season is winter. The effects guys took a flocking machine up on a crane and let the snow rain down so it hung on everything like real snow does. Then we used another variation of snow, like peeled plastic chips, that blows around during the scene. It looks great—it's a mess.

"Besides all the horses, they had real wolves onstage during this scene. Then everyone had to stand real still, because any movement scares them."

Opposite and above: *The battle between gypsies and Vampire Killers reaches the castle.*

On Dracula's box
in the foreground, the battle going on in the background. We see the rim of the sun. We move in on the box.

Insert—sun very near the horizon

[Dracula's box—continuing action]

Dracula in the earth
Shifting positions, head and hands. The night begins to stir the warrior awake. A name forms on his parched lips: "Mina."

[Castle promontory—sunset]

Medium shot Mina
She turns to camera and we track into her closeup; she reacts to hearing her name called.

[Borgo Road—sunset]

The fast-moving battle continues.

Medium wide shot
Mina turns and starts climbing up the formation toward the castle gates. She lifts her hands and chants, calling up the winds. The sky darkens.

Insert—gathering storm clouds

Van Helsing
Madam Mina! Wait!

He follows her.

[Dracula's box]

Dracula surges with power. A smile of triumph spreads on his face.

[Borgo Road—sunset]

Wide shot
Nearing the castle. Hard winds come up and literally blow Harker's horse over.

Harker hits the ground
Quincey circles around and pulls him up on his horse. They ride double in pursuit.

View on the sun
Last rays of the sun. Very cold; snow falls. Music in.

Side angle profile
on Harker and Quincey as they ride up to the moving wagon. Harker leaps aboard. Quincey stays on the horse, close behind—

Low angle
The Gypsy Driver lashes at Harker with his whip. Holmwood drops him with a shot from behind. The driver falls.

[Tunnel entrance—sunset]

Camera on wagon
behind Harker and the box. The wagon enters the tunnel, roaring by Mina and Van Helsing, and comes to a screeching halt in the courtyard.

View into the tunnel
Quincey, Seward, and Holmwood ride through the tunnel, firing at the two remaining Szgany. One drops.

[Castle courtyard—continuing action]

Holmwood wheels in place
at the tunnel entrance, picking off gypsies with expert shots as they appear along the crumbling ramparts.

Seward runs a gypsy through,
protecting Mina and Van Helsing.

Harker on the wagon
He slashes at the bonds holding the box. One gypsy jumps at him and they fight on the wagon. Wolves attack.

On Quincey
He jumps to rescue Harker, but a gypsy slashes him in the back. He falls and fights hand-to-hand—bleeding profusely.

Back on wagon
Harker swings his kukri and finishes the gypsy.

Mina and Van Helsing
Mina running in horror, to camera. Van Helsing tries to hold her back. Wolves howl all around them.

View on their shadows
elongating as the sun sets, its last rays striking the Borgo Road.

Dracula's box
It quakes—then the lid explodes, smashing over Harker. Dracula rises and grabs Harker by the throat, roaring like a beast.

Above: *Quincey stabs Dracula with his giant Bowie knife, whose elaborate hilt is shown in silhouette on page 163.*

Reverse on Harker
He swings his kukri, cutting Dracula's neck.

On the ground
Crimson blood spatters pure white snow. (Music cue.)

Medium closeup Mina
screaming in horror.

Quincey dives, driving his Bowie knife deep into Dracula's heart. Dracula roars, flinging Quincey into the snow. (Music cue: chanting prayers.)

Dracula in the snow
He writhes, clawing at the knife. A great beast is dying. He stands erect, facing his assailants, blood streaming from his severed throat—the Bowie knife stuck deep in his chest.

On Mina
She rushes to Dracula, aiming her Winchester wildly at Harker—then Seward—Holmwood—

View on the men
all shocked by her action.

HARKER
(*horrified*)
Mina!

Mina and Dracula
Dracula turns to her. His face horribly transformed.

DRACULA
(*tender, loving*)
Mina . . .?

She holds his dying gaze. He turns and drags himself toward the chapel. Mina backs slowly after him, her gun on the men.

MINA
When my time comes—will you do the same to me? *Will you?*

On men over Mina
Holmwood looking at her, the rifle pointing at him. Harker, loving her, begins to understand. Holmwood tries to rush to her. Harker holds him back, understanding Mina's resolve.

HARKER
No, let them go. Let her go. Our work is finished here . . . hers is just begun.

Closeup Van Helsing
nods knowingly. Harker has learned from his nightmare.

Closeup Mina
She aims pointblank at Harker.

On Harker over Mina
She fires! We pull back to see a wolf leaping from the ramparts at him, crashing to the ground—dead.

Back to Mina and Dracula
Mina backs after Dracula into the castle, never taking her eyes or her gun off the men.

[Chapel door—sunset]

Medium wide shot
Harker waits at the chapel door nervously. Holmwood is pacing, pounding his fists futilely against it. Van Helsing holds his hand up, indicating that they should be still.

Seward cradles Quincey
He dies. . . .

Costume designer Eiko Ishioka:

"In depicting the 1890s, we needed to show that it was an age when men were very macho. And Transylvania was a land of fiercely cold climate. So the 'Five Samurai' were dressed accordingly. The nobleman Holmwood in a fur mantle. The young executive Harker in a long leather coat. The ascetic Dr. Seward in a grey quilt. The rich Texan Quincey in a leather cowboy coat. And the profound scientist Van Helsing in an elegant cape. Mina is the reincarnation of a 15th-century princess, so I designed her cape in the last scene with a strong Renaissance flavor."

Francis Coppola says, "I had set myself the task of trying to find someone to play Dracula who was basically young and a great actor, and capable of expressing passion." He found his title character in Gary Oldman.

Winona Ryder, who tested with Oldman, remembers, "He had a real character in his head already. It was startling."

Associate producer Susie Landau also recalls the screen tests "As we were watching Gary's playback, we got chills. It was singular and mercurial. He had a tremendous weariness, which none of the other actors who read for the part had. Dracula has been around for 400 years. He's totally isolated and lonely, and Gary made that real."

Born in 1958 in London, Gary Oldman first encountered Dracula at age five when he masqueraded as the vampire at a fancy-dress contest. The actor's serious theatrical career began in drama school and regional theater; later he moved on to the London stage at the Royal Court Theatre. He originated the role of Corman in *Serious Money* and won the 1985 British Theatre Association's Drama Magazine Award for his performance in *The Pope's Wedding*. The award was shared that year—for the first time in its history—with Anthony Hopkins.

Oldman has also performed with the Royal Shakespeare Company and in British TV dramas. His film roles include punk-rocker Sid Vicious in *Sid and Nancy*, playwright Joe Orton in *Prick Up Your Ears*, and most recently, Lee Harvey Oswald in *JFK*.

Known for his intense preparation, Oldman researched Dracula in numerous books. But his chief insights about vampires came from Anne Rice's *Interview with the Vampire*. The novel left him with the sense that vampires do exist but are not happy with their immortal fate. "Vampires are fascinating. They are selfish, destructive creatures who half despise what they're doing yet can't avoid doing it."

Oldman came to see his character as fallen angel, a tortured soul. "I don't play him as out-and-out evil. It's a delicious cocktail because you know he is like the devil. But I've tried to show the good and bad paralleling one another—there's a dynamic there.

"The film image I can't get away from is Bela Lugosi. He was really on to something: the way he moved, the way he sounded. I based my voice on his a little."

Vocal preparation was just one of the skills Oldman had to practice for Dracula, working with a vocal coach to lower the register of his voice almost an octave. He also had a dialogue coach for his accent, and a Romanian teacher to learn scenes in that language. He studied dancing and swordsmanship, spent hours in costume fittings and the makeup chair.

Though rehearsals went on for weeks, Oldman resisted the temptation to simply "mark" the part and didn't hold back on intensity. "I think if you're essentially a leading man, you have to rally the troops," he asserts. "You've got to get a sense of what you and the other actors are going to do. The only way I could get into this part was to go for it. The scenes where I was howling or screaming—you have to really prepare for it physically."

As he descended into the role, other cast members found him scary at times, especially during an improvisation exercise suggested by Coppola. In the scene where Dracula as the bat creature confronts the Vampire Killers, Oldman was having trouble. He felt trapped in the costume: how could he feel his supernatural power over them?

"Francis felt they didn't look frightened enough. So he blindfolded the cast and told me to go and whisper in the ear of each one—something horrible and personal and scary." Oldman followed directions with relish, and his fellow actors were chilled and repelled.

Yet the other side of Dracula was never far away. Screenwriter Jim Hart says, "Gary told me he was most comfortable in the old-age character because when you're old, you've survived. As dark as the role can be, he has brought compassion and a tenderness to it that people haven't seen in Dracula before. My heart breaks for him, you know?"

On Van Helsing
He drops his gun and faces the chapel. He bows his head, praying intensely.

VAN HELSING
Rest him. Let him sleep in peace. . . .We have all become God's mad men.

[Castle chapel—sunset]

Wide shot
Dracula and Mina on the altar steps. Deep in the caverns of his eyes, fierce life still burns. We track in on them.

DRACULA
Where is my God? He forsakes me.

Mina grips the handle of the knife and tries to pull it out. His fingers, nearly bone, creep up the shaft, stopping her.

DRACULA
It is finished.

Filled with love, she stares down into his eyes. She cradles him, kissing him, smoothing his matted, graying hair. Suddenly she speaks intimately in Roumanian—he responds.

MINA
No . . . my love—

He shudders, blood welling up from the wound in his heart.

DRACULA
Give me peace.

View on the steps—high overhead angle
Old candles light themselves. The shadow of the crucifix moves across the floor as Mina, glowing, moves into the place and manner as when Elizabeth lay there.

Dracula raises his eyes to . . . Elizabeth. Camera starts slowly booming down.

She rises up and kisses him. Camera moves closer. His youth is restored. She comforts him. He puts her hand on the knife in his heart. Mina's hands on the knife. She quakes, knowing what she must do. She closes her eyes, prays for strength, and falls on him with all her weight, driving the knife clear through his heart.

Close shot—the knife
The steel point penetrating the ground.

Medium close shot
Mina cradling Dracula. His eyes go up—he sleeps . . . peacefully, beautifully, as a human.

View on the crucifix
The impalement mark heals itself, disappearing.

Medium closeup Mina
The ruins echo with her tender weeping. She rises. The mark on her forehead is gone. She is free. . .

Medium wide shot—chapel door
It is snowing. Harker opens the door and looks in. He is overjoyed to see Mina well. She rushes to him in an embrace. He holds her, understanding what has happened.

View cranes
to the top of the magnificent altar, as they leave.

Mina sends her prince to his rest.

[Chapel interior—sunset]

Close shot
The dragon arch, illuminating his name—
"DRACULEA"

[Castle courtyard—sunset]
The Warrior Prince is at peace.

[Great hall—sunset]

High angle—Mina and Harker
walking across the restored mosaic of the cross. They are followed by Van Helsing, Seward, and Holmwood, carrying the body of Quincey.

Van Helsing speaks in voiceover:

"We want no proofs. We ask none to believe us. God be thanked that all has not been in vain—the curse has passed away."
(Bram Stoker)

Columbia Pictures Presents
An American Zoetrope / Osiris Films Production

Columbia Pictures Presents

BRAM STOKER'S

A FRANCIS FORD COPPOLA FILM

GARY OLDMAN as Dracula

WINONA RYDER as Mina Harker

ANTHONY HOPKINS as Abraham Van Helsing

KEANU REEVES as Jonathan Harker

SADIE FROST as Lucy Westenra

RICHARD E. GRANT as Dr. Jack Seward

CARY ELWES as Arthur Holmwood

BILL CAMPBELL as Quincey Morris

and

TOM WAITS as Renfield

Directed by FRANCIS FORD COPPOLA

Screenplay by JAMES V. HART

Produced by FRANCIS FORD COPPOLA, FRED FUCHS, AND
CHARLES MULVEHILL

Executive Producers MICHAEL APTED
AND ROBERT O'CONNOR

Director of Photography MICHAEL BALLHAUS, A.S.C.

Production Designer THOMAS SANDERS

Edited by NICHOLAS C. SMITH, GLENN SCANTLEBURY,
AND ANNE GOURSAUD, A.C.E.

Costumes Designed by EIKO ISHIOKA

Music by WOJCIECH KILAR

Visual Effects ROMAN COPPOLA

Casting by VICTORIA THOMAS

Co-Producer JAMES V. HART

Associate Producer SUSIE LANDAU

Dracula: The King Vampire

by Leonard Wolf

In 1997, the Count Dracula invented by Irish novelist Bram Stoker in 1897 will be one hundred years old. With Francis Ford Coppola's new film rendering of the story in 1992, we have proof once again of the wily and sinister old vampire's incredible hold on our imaginations.

In America literally hundreds of products using his name or his story have been marketed: recordings, sweatshirts, jigsaw puzzles, Halloween candy, lapel buttons, furniture, and hair oil. Even a children's cereal, Count Chocula, waits in the supermarket to entice the Sesame Street set, who have also learned to count in his name.

For young children who are not precisely aware of what Dracula does for a living, his attraction may be simply that he is easy to turn into a cartoon image of all that is sinister. Make him tall and cadaverously pale,

Right: Max Schreck as Count Orlok, on board the Demeter *in Murnau's 1922 film* Nosferatu. *Opposite: Bela Lugosi in the 1931 Universal* Dracula.

give him a long black cloak lined in red silk, and let him say, "I vant to drink your blood," and youngsters have both the thrill of recognition and a bad guy who is part scary, part comic.

But for adults the Dracula matter is considerably more complex. We want to know where he comes from and why he has such a persistent hold on our pysches. We want to understand how a character described by his inventor as an old man with a drooping white mustache, bad breath, and hair on his palms has been transformed into a continental aristocrat who steps out of his coffin suavely to seduce desirable women. But most of all, we want to know why he continues to fascinate us.

To get at the lure of Dracula to the contemporary imagination, we have to glance briefly at the literary tradition to which Bram Stoker's novel belongs. *Dracula* is a late Victorian example of the Gothic novel, which, from the time of its origin in eighteenth-century England, was meant to scare its readers. The typical Gothic fiction featured a beautiful, young, well-bred heroine and a tall, dark villain whose intentions were strictly dishonorable. The genre is called Gothic because the heroine was usually pursued through dark, dismal places like ruined monasteries, castles, fortresses, caverns, or grisly mausoleums. The most typical of the novels is Ann Radcliffe's *The Mysteries of Udolpho* (1794); the most vivid is still Matthew Lewis's *The Monk* (1796); while the most profound is Charles Maturin's *Melmoth the Wanderer* (1820).

What must be noted about Gothic fiction is that from the start it linked a wide range of erotic experience with fear. Gothic novels accommodated themes of incest, perversion, and sexual violence that were either missing from or treated at arm's length in mainstream fiction. Also from the beginning, Gothic villains (and villainesses) were members of the nobility or otherwise people of wealth or power.

We have such a villain in the first vampire fiction in English. In his 1819 novel *The Vampyre*, John Polidori gives us the prototype of the vampire as he will almost invariably be presented thereafter in literature and film. Polidori's vampire is a nobleman named Lord Ruthven, who is the nemesis of his friend, young Aubrey, the tale's hero. Ruthven, we are told, has a deadly hue, a cold eye, and a base heart, yet nevertheless is fascinating to women. Killed by an encounter with bandits, he is restored to life when his corpse is exposed by the unsuspecting Aubrey to the light of a full moon, after which the vampire is free to resume his deadly career—and the destruction of Aubrey's sister.

Sheridan LeFanu's short novel *Carmilla* (1872) is an altogether more impressive vampire fiction. For one thing, LeFanu, unlike Polidori, is a literary craftsman who wields a subtle, if sedate, prose whose very civility heightens the horror of his tale. His nineteen-year-old narrator recounts her nearly fatal experience with the beautiful vampire Carmilla, who, in her various manifestations as the Countess Mercalla and Millarca, has terrorized a Styrian province for more than a century. *Carmilla* is a worthy precursor to Stoker's *Dracula* in that it makes careful use of vampire folklore and because, in the midst of the Victorian age, LeFanu saw clearly the link between eroticism and the vampire theme. He writes:

> The vampire is prone to be fascinated with an engrossing vehemence, resembling the passion of love, by particular persons. . . . It will never desist until it has satiated its passion and drained the very life of its coveted victim.

"Resembling the passion of love." There's the heart of the matter. Stoker's

achievement is that he has created an adventure story whose chief image—an undead creature who drinks the blood of attractive young women—shimmers with erotic meanings. The blood exchanges in *Dracula*, and the extraordinary eroticism with which Stoker describes them, are what make it such an amazing book.

Early reviews of the book failed to make much of this point, but it was not long before the film industry got the message. In *Nosferatu*, F. W. Murnau's 1922 silent screen adaptation, the vampire is called Count Orlok. Near the conclusion of that still compelling film its heroine, Nina, flings open her bedroom window and welcomes the vampire. While the camera work that follows is remarkably unspecific, it clearly suggests a couple—one of whom is engrossed in while the other is enduring an act of love.

Cover illustration from Varney the Vampyre *(this variant spelling was used in the actual title), a potboiler serial by James Malcolm Rymer, 1847.*

Since *Nosferatu*, the eroticism of vampire imagery has continued to haunt movie screens, as filmmakers and audiences have grasped that the blood scenes are also implicitly love scenes. More than any earlier film, Coppola's *Dracula* makes this meaning explicit. The blood exchange also has represented all the ways, permitted and taboo, that mankind has found to make love. "[The vampire's] kiss permits all unions: men and women, men and men; women and women; fathers and daughters; mothers and sons. Moreover, his is an easy love that evades the usual failures of the flesh." (From *A Dream of Dracula*.)

The very first performance of *Dracula* was a one-time staged reading at the Lyceum Theatre in London, meant simply to establish Stoker's theatrical copyright. The first dramatically viable performance of *Dracula* as a play took place in England in 1925, in a version made by Hamilton Deane. It was an immediate success, but the tide of public interest in the King Vampire really began to flow in 1927, when the American publisher Horace Liveright got John Balderston to create with Deane a revised version of the play. The Deane-Balderston version, with all its weaknesses, is the one most frequently performed.

There have been other theatrical versions of *Dracula*. Orson Welles dramatized it for a Mercury Theater radio production in 1938. In 1980, Leon Katz's *Dracula: Sabbat*, a highly stylized play with almost no relationship to Stoker's work, appeared on Broadway, and in 1971 Ted Tiller's *Count Dracula* proved successful in regional and college theaters. But it is the Deane-Balderston play that—according to one of Stoker's biographers—is still playing somewhere every day of the year.

In February 1931, Universal Studios released its version of *Dracula*. The film, directed by Tod Browning, was based on the Balderston-Deane play and starred Bela Lugosi as Dracula. By now it is nearly received opinion that the Browning *Dracula* is not a great film. Its narrative line is fitful

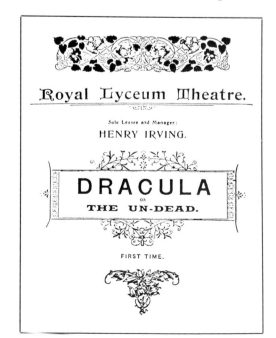

Royal Lyceum Theatre.

Sole Lessee and Manager:
HENRY IRVING.

DRACULA
OR
THE UN-DEAD.

FIRST TIME.

and it is marred by low-comedy interludes; still, the film has achieved classic status for good reason. It has some of the most sinister Gothic sets ever made. It has the suavely grim photography of Karl Freund. It has Edward Van Sloan playing Dr. Van Helsing and Dwight Frye as Renfield, laughing the most terrifying laugh ever recorded in movies. And however one may characterize Lugosi's performance—cold, remote, hokey—it conveys nevertheless the authority of evil and its fatal attraction. That, his accent, and his impeccable evening clothes have turned his Dracula into an enduring icon of evil.

The number of films using the name Dracula or exploiting the Dracula theme now runs into several hundred. Here I want to notice a few that I find memorable (though not necessarily great). In my view, the best of the Universal sequels is *Dracula's Daughter* (1936), starring Gloria Holden in the title role and Edward Van Sloan once again as Van Helsing. Garrett Fort's script tells the tragic story of Countess Dracula, who, after consigning her father's body to the flames, tries with psychiatric help to rid herself of the curse of vampirism. But blood will tell, as they say, and she is her father's daughter. When her vampirism resurfaces, she kidnaps her psychiatrist's fiancée and flies with her to Transylvania in order to get the psychiatrist, with whom she is in love, to follow her. *Dracula's Daughter* is notable for its theme of vampire loneliness and for the poignant and mythic manner in which the story is told.

Billy the Kid Versus Dracula (1965) appeared around the time that "camp" was coming into vogue. No one can or should take the film seriously. At the same time, no one should miss seeing the great actor John Carradine good-humoredly spoofing himself and the vampire genre. Dracula in cowboy country is already more than half the joke.

After Lugosi and before Gary Oldman in Coppola's 1992 *Dracula*, there have been only two other substantial interpreters of Dracula in the movies: Christopher Lee in various Hammer Film exploitations of the character (*The Horror of Dracula*, 1958; *Dracula—Prince of Darkness*, 1965; and oth-

ers) and Frank Langella's performance in Universal's 1979 *Dracula*, directed by John Badham. Lee's characterizations are notable for the quality of dangerous stillness he gives the King Vampire, while Langella, taking Dracula's eroticism for granted, plays him as so utterly good-looking, charming, and desirable that it is hard to imagine any woman being frightened of his embrace. Gary Oldman, the most recent interpreter, plays the role as Stoker first created it: first as a man so old he seems to embody ancient evil, and then, as he is nourished by his victim's blood, as a dashing young seducer.

But there is more to the appeal of the Dracula image than its hidden or overt eroticism. The story—indeed, the theme of vampirism itself—has embedded in it a religious component. The usual monsters of folklore or filmdom are of course dangerous, but the vampire taking the blood of his victim is a threat to both body and soul. This is what makes the already engaging struggle between good guys and bad take on the larger meaning of a fight between the cohorts of God and those of Satan. This religious component also gives filmmakers a welcome opportunity to play out their fictions against a background of mysterious rituals and majestic pomp.

Finally, one must call attention to a thin but important line of meaning in the Dracula story. Van Helsing tells us that the universal unbelief in the existence of vampires makes it hard for us to recognize them, thus enhancing their power. The truth may be deeper and more disturbing. Readers and filmgoers recognize that Dracula is attractive precisely because he represents the dark side of our own natures. We live in an age that admires energy and power, and we know more about erotic fantasies than may be good for us. No wonder we look up in fear at Dracula, who is forever charged with energy and suffused with power, and who acts out his atrocious fantasies. No wonder we are glad to see him stopped—in film after film, forever.

✠

Further Reading and Viewing

A limited selection of books about the Dracula phenomenon that are currently available or were used in preparing this book, and some of the more noteworthy film adaptations, as recommended by Francis Ford Coppola, James Hart, and Leonard Wolf.

BOOKS

Coppola, Francis Ford, Ishioka Eiko, and Seidner, David, edited by Susan Dworkin. *Coppola and Eiko on Bram Stoker's Dracula*. San Francisco: Collins San Francisco, 1992.

Deane, Hamilton, and Balderston, John. *Dracula: The Vampire Play in Three Acts*. New York: Samuel French, Inc., 1960.

Farson, Daniel. *The Man Who Wrote Dracula: A Biography of Bram Stoker*. New York: St. Martin's Press, 1976.

Florescu, Radu R. and McNally, Raymond T. *Dracula: Prince of Many Faces*. Boston: Little, Brown & Co., 1989.

_____. *In Search of Dracula*. Greenwich, Connecticut: New York Graphic Society, 1972.

Frayling, Christopher. *Vampyres: Lord Byron to Count Dracula*. London: Faber and Faber Limited, 1991.

Ludlum, Harry. *A Biography of Dracula: The Life Story of Bram Stoker*. London: Foulsham, 1962.

Riley, Philip J., ed. *Dracula: The Original 1931 Shooting Script*. Atlantic City and Hollywood: MagicImage Filmbooks, 1990.

Saberhagen, Fred and Hart, James V., based on the screenplay by James V. Hart *Bram Stoker's Dracula: The Novel of the Film Directed by Francis Ford Coppola*. New York: Signet/Penguin USA, and Pan Books (UK), 1992.

Skal, David J. *Hollywood Gothic: The Tangled Web of Dracula from Novel to Stage to Screen*. New York: W.W. Norton & Co., 1990.

Stoker, Bram. *Dracula*. London: Constable & Co., 1897. Reissued in an official movie tie-in edition by Signet/Penguin USA and Pan Books (UK), 1992.

Thomas, Roy, ed., Mignola, Mike and Nyberg, John. *Bram Stoker's Dracula: The Official Comics Adaptation*. Brooklyn, N.Y.: Topps Comics, Inc., 1992.

Wolf, Leonard. *A Dream of Dracula*. Boston: Little, Brown & Co., 1972.

Wolf, Leonard, ed. *The Annotated Dracula, by Bram Stoker*. New York: Clarkson N. Potter, Inc., 1975. Republished with new material as *The Essential Dracula*. New York: Plume Books/Penguin USA, 1993.

FILMS

1922 *Nosferatu*. F. W. Murnau, director, Prana Films, Germany. Starring Max Schreck as Count Orlok. Unauthorized, loosely adapted classic of German Expressionist cinema.

1931 *Dracula*. Tod Browning, director, Universal Pictures. Starring Bela Lugosi as Count Dracula. The best-known version, Lugosi's film debut in his alter ego role after playing Dracula on the stage.

1936 *Dracula's Daughter*. Lambert Hillyer, director, Universal. Starring Gloria Holden as Countess Zaleska. See Afterword.

1943 *Son of Dracula*. Robert Siodmak, director, Universal. Starring Lon Chaney Jr. as Count Alucard. First American setting for a vampire tale.

1945 *House of Dracula*. Erle C. Kenton, director, Universal. Starring John Carradine as Count Dracula. Carradine's first appearance as Dracula.

1958 *The Horror of Dracula*. Terence Fisher, director, Hammer Film, England. Starring Christopher Lee as Count Dracula. Best of the several Lee incarnations.

1965 *Billy the Kid vs. Dracula*. Terence Fisher, director, Hammer Film, England. Christopher Lee again; see Afterword.

1969 *The Fearless Vampire Killers*. Roman Polanski, director, Cadre-MGM. Starring Ferdy Mayne as Count Von Krolok. Minimal resemblance to the Dracula story, but a fine spoof of the genre.

1974 *Dracula*. Andy Warhol and Paul Morrissey, directors, Carlo Ponti-Braunsberg Rassam Productions. Starring Udo Kier as Count Dracula.

1979 *Nosferatu*. Werner Herzog, director, Filmproduktion/ Beaumont, Germany. Starring Klaus Kinski as Count Orlok. Herzog's color remake of the Murnau classic is a visual *tour de force*.

1979 *Dracula*. John Badham, director, Mirisch Corporation for Universal Pictures. Starring Frank Langella as Dracula. Langella recreates his sexy stage performance in a lush screen production.

1992 *Bram Stoker's Dracula*. Francis Ford Coppola, director, Columbia Pictures. Starring Gary Oldman as Prince Vlad Dracula.

About the Authors

FRANCIS FORD COPPOLA

Writer/director/producer Francis Coppola most recently completed *Godfather III*, the last chapter in his three-part trilogy on the Corleone family. Coppola's other credits include the *Life Without Zoe* episode of *New York Stories, Tucker: The Man and His Dream, Gardens of Stone, Peggy Sue Got Married, Cotton Club, Rumble Fish, The Outsiders, One From the Heart, Apocalypse Now, The Conversation, The Rain People,* and *You're a Big Boy Now.*

Coppola, who is the son of composer Carmine Coppola, was born in Detroit and grew up in New York. After earning his MFA from the film school at UCLA, he apprenticed with low-budget impresario Roger Corman as a soundman, dialogue director, associate producer, and screenwriter before he wrote and directed his first feature, *Dementia 13*, in 1963. For the next several years he was involved in production work and script collaborations while directing his own screenplays for several films. His work on *Patton* with Edmund H. North earned him an Oscar for Best Screenplay Adaptation.

In 1970 he and George Lucas established American Zoetrope; its first production, *THX-1138*, was directed by Lucas and produced by Coppola. Coppola also produced Lucas's *American Graffiti* and has been executive producer on several notable films including *The Black Stallion*, Akira Kurosawa's *Kagemusha*, and Paul Schrader's *Mishima*.

Coppola's most honored films are *Apocalypse Now* (the Palme d'Or at Cannes and two Academy Awards) and the Godfather trilogy, which has earned numerous Oscars including Best Picture for *The Godfather*. He is Chairman of American Zoetrope, the San Francisco-based production company infused with his creative spirit, and the proprietor of Niebaum-Coppola Estate Winery in the Napa Valley, where the Coppola family makes its home.

JAMES V. HART

Screenwriter and co-producer Jim Hart spent a lot of time on Sony Studios sound stages in 1991, as the spectacular sets for his first produced script, *Hook*, were built and then dismantled to make way for production of *Bram Stoker's Dracula*. Now living in New York, Hart was born in Shreveport, Louisiana, and brought up in Texas. He attended Southern Methodist University, majoring in finance and economics, and was working on his master's degree in broadcast film arts at SMU when he began producing low-budget "drive-in" movies, the first of which was *Summer Run*.

In 1970 Hart and a filmmaker friend drove his VW bus from Fort Worth to San Francisco on the chance of meeting Francis Ford Coppola. After they waited all day at the Zoetrope building, the director appeared. His advice to the young Texans: keep making movies.

Hart began writing in earnest in the late 1970s, tackling his first *Dracula* adaptation in 1977. He persevered through various frustrating development deals until *Hook*, and then *Dracula*, became a reality. With Hart's future as a writer now assured, he is turning his sights toward directing.

LEONARD WOLF

Born in Vulcan, Romania (in Transylvania), Leonard Wolf is the author of *The Annotated Dracula* (republished as *The Essential Dracula*) and *A Dream of Dracula*. His work in the horror genre has been honored twice with the Anne Radcliffe Award for Literature. Wolf served as technical consultant to the film.

A published author of poems, short stories, and two novels, Wolf is also a Yiddish translator and the designated biographer of Isaac Bashevis Singer, for Farrar, Straus and Giroux. He now lives in New York City.

Acknowledgments

Permission to reprint copyrighted material from the following sources is gratefully acknowledged. The publisher has made all reasonable efforts to contact copyright holders for permission; any errors in the form of credit given will be corrected in future printings.

Absinthe: History in a Bottle, by Barnaby Conrad III (Chronicle Books). Copyright © 1988 by Barnaby Conrad III.

Academy of Motion Picture Arts and Sciences: Photographs of Christopher Lee in *Dracula Has Risen from the Grave*, © 1968 Warner Bros.-Seven Arts, Inc.; Bela Lugosi and Dracula's Wives in *Dracula*, © 1931 Universal Pictures Company, Inc., copyright renewed 1958.

Photograph from the film *Beauty and the Beast*, directed by Jean Cocteau.

The Book Sail, Orange, California, and John McLaughlin: Page from Bram Stoker's working manuscript for *Dracula*.

Ronald V. Borst/Hollywood Movie Posters: Photographs of Frank Langella, Bram Stoker, *Varney The Vampire* book cover, and Max Schreck in *Nosferatu* (1922).

Historisches Museum der Stadt Wein, Vienna: *Tragedy*, painting by Gustav Klimt, c. 1897, black chalk heightened with white and gold, 41.9 x 30.8.

Hollywood Gothic: The Tangled Web of Dracula from Novel to Stage to Screen, by David J. Skal (W.W. Norton & Company). Copyright © 1990 by Visual Cortex Ltd. For: *Nosferatu* poster by Albin Grau (Anthology Film Archives collection); 1916 *Dracula* book jacket (Robert James Leake Collection); *The Vampire*, painting by Philip Burne-Jones; cover of Lyceum Theatre program and *Dracula's Guest* book jacket (Jeanne Youngson Collection).

In Search of Dracula, by Radu R. Florescu and Raymond T. McNally. Reprinted by permission of Little, Brown and Company. Copyright © 1972 by Raymond T. McNally and Radu Florescu. For: Map of Transylvania and Wallachia, photograph of Castle Bran.

Photograph from *Ivan the Terrible*, *Part One* (1944), directed by Sergei Eisenstein.

Kunstmuseum, Vienna Portrait of Vlad Tepes from Castle Ambras, Austria.

Library of the Academy of Romania, Bucharest: Engraving of Brasov.

Musée de Pontarlier, France: Anti-absinthe lithograph by Stop.

Museo d'Arte Moderna, Cà Pesaro, Venice: *Judith II*, painting by Gustav Klimt, c. 1909, oil on canvas, 178 x 46.

Muzeum Adama Mickiewicza, Warsaw: *Obsession*, painting by Wojciech Weiss, c. 1899-1900, oil on canvas, 100 x 185.

Narodní Gallery, Prague: Resistance: *The Black Idol*, aquatint by Frantisek Kupka.

Staatsbibliothek, Colmar, Germany: Woodcut of impalement scene.

Martha Swope Photography: Photograph of Frank Langella in the 1977 stage revival of *Dracula*.

Leonard Wolf: Drawings by Satty from *The Annotated Dracula*.

All photographs from the film by Ralph Nelson with the following exceptions: pages 40 and 60, by Fabian Cevallos; pages 153 and 158, by Steve Schapiro.

We thank the following for their special contributions: at American Zoetrope, Anahid Nazarian, who directed us to sources, loaned materials, and provided vital information in response to countless inquiries; Susie Landau and Fred Fuchs, who reviewed and oversaw this book's progress; Kim Aubry, Roman Coppola, Mara Hamilton, Nick Smith, and Steve Weisman. At Columbia Pictures and Sony Studios, Katherine Orloff, who was a critical link at all stages and whose research served as key source material; Bradley Blasdel, who cheerfully helped us ransack the prop warehouse; Helen LaVarre and Boyd Peterson, for their help with photographs; and Lester Borden, Diane Burstein, Susan Christison, Sidney Ganis, Mark Gill, Marcy Granata, Diane Salerno, and Randy Smith, for their invaluable marketing and creative support.

Also the staffs of Walking Stick Press and Newmarket Press for their unflagging commitment to excellence despite scheduling challenges, Susan Dworkin for her research on costumes, Jeff Werner and Docula Productions, Davia Nelson, Judy Mason, Catherine Quittner, Pam Earing, Greg Miller, and Damien Niño.

We owe special thanks to James V. Hart for his epic screenplay, his commitment in bringing the real Dracula to the screen, and his notes on the experience that appear here; to Leonard Wolf for his enlightening Afterword and all his stimulating writing on the vampire theme; to the producers, Francis Ford Coppola, Fred Fuchs, and Charles Mulvehill, for their achievement in creating *Bram Stocker's Dracula* and their support of our book about it; and especially to Francis Coppola for contributing his personal history as a Dracula fan and his fascinating comments on the making of this extraordinary film.